P. Müller and W. Rumpf

Modern World
Fact and Fiction

Volume II:
Man and Mat
Man against Man

Lehrerbegleitband

manz

MANZ VERLAG MÜNCHEN

Herausgegeben von Ute Kretschmann

Manzbuch 538

6 5 4 3 2 1 1989 88 87 86
(Die jeweils letzte Zahl bezeichnet die Auflage bzw. das Erscheinungsjahr)

Umschlagentwurf: Ingeburg Rothemund, München
Gesamtherstellung: Verlag und Druckerei G. J. Manz AG, München/Dillingen
Printed in Germany

ISBN 3-7863-0538-2

TABLE OF CONTENTS

I. SURVEY OF TOPICS AND WORKSHEETS

(ws = worksheet)

Title	Topic	Language	Grammar	Literature	Varia
1: Should Women Fight in War? (Interview)	Sex roles – equality of man and woman	Word groups (ws 1.1) Collocations (1.2) synonyms (1.3) idioms (1.4)	– –	Analysis and interpretation of comic strips (Introducing the Topic; ws 4.1) "The Scarlet Letter": research paper (4.3)	Interpretation of picture (Introducing the Topic ws 8) essay writing (4.2)
2: Facial Justice (Excerpt from a novel)	Equality: an idea driven ad absurdum	For your reading pleasure	– –	Anti-utopia; comparison with *Brave New World* and *1984*	Cartoon
3: Fear of Flying (Excerpt from a novel)	Emancipation of the woman	Paraphrase (ws 1.1) collocations (1.2)	Relative clauses (teacher's book)	– –	Wordgames (1.3; 1.4); reading, verbalizing, and completing a chart (3.6); making up of conversation; analysis of a cartoon

Title	Topic	Language	Grammar	Literature	Varia
4: The Perfect Woman (Short story)	Man creates woman in his image	Grammatical homonym (ws 1.1) characteristics of the English language: flexibility and malleability (1.1); word families: equal, please, suffer, construct, perceive, perfect (1.2); semantic fields; drink, eat, think, walk, laugh (1.3)	– –	– –	Cartoon (4.1) jokes (4.2)
5: A legal, Moral, Social Nightmare (Magazine article)	Moral and legal implications of the "birth revolution" (in-vitro fertili-zation – surrogacy)	Word families; antonyms, synonyms, paraphrases (ws 1.1 + 1.2); "fill-in-the- gaps"-exercises (1.3 + 1.5) collocations (1.4)	– –	– –	The use of index cards (1.1 + 1.2) research paper (3.)
6: Problems of the Family Today Newspaper headlines and clippings)	Violence in the family	Word group: familiy rela-tionship (ws 1.1 + 1.2); explanation of phrases (1.3); nouns ending in -ee and -er/or (1.4); word group "court proceedings" (1.5)	– –	Song; analysis of newspapers (2.6 + 2.7); analysis of news, newspaper headlines, letter to the editor	Listening comprehension exercise; reading and verbalizing of diagrams (Introducing the Topic; ws 2.4); role play (3.4)

Title	Topic	Language	Grammar	Literature	Varia
					writing a letter to the editor (3.1 + 3.2); research paper (3.5); project word (4.)
7: Brave New World (Excerpt from a novel)	Future society without families	Prefix "be-"; countries and their languages (ws 1.1); "Enrich your word power": homonyms (ws 1.3); Terms and their counterparts (1.4)	– –	– –	– –
8: Hunger Is . . . (Advertisement)	Anti-hunger campaigns and their consequences	Translating into English (6a)	– –	Analysis of advertisement	Writing of letters to the editor (5c, 6b);
9: Overcoming Overpopulation and Starvation in Underdeveloped Countries (Excerpt from a social study)	Ways of changing UDCs into S(emi)DCs	Negating prefixes (1.1); paraphrases (1.2); Americanisms (1.3); spelling of homophones (1.4); story writing (1.5); analysis of style and speech level (2.2.2); analysis of text type (2.2.3)	– –	– –	Reading and verbalizing a chart (Introducing the Topic); Interpreting a cartoon (4.)

Title	Topic	Language	Grammar	Literature	Varia
10: The Wanting Seed excerpt from a novel)	Overpopulation in GB	Synonyms (ws 1.1); paraphrases (1.2)	Absolute participles (teacher's book); reflexives (teacher's book)	– –	– –
11: Castaway (Excerpt from an account)	Human behaviour in unusual situations and under stress	Preposition exercises (1.1 + 1.2); phrasal verbs: to put + particles (1.3); translation exercise (3.1)	Analysis of grammatical structures: rel. clauses; gerund; participle; infinitive; passive clauses; change of word class (3.1.1)	Comparison of *Castaway* with *Robinson Crusoe*	Crossword puzzle (1.4); map (reading and comment) (3.2)
12: Lord of the Flies (Excerpt from a novel)	Extreme situation; human aggression	Language game (ws 1.1); error recognition exercise (1.2 + 1.3); true – false exercise (2.2)	– –	*Lord of the Flies* – *Robinson Crusoe* – *Coral Island:* a comparison	Theories on human aggression (German text for English gist) [4.2]
13: Dreaming that Dream (Excerpt from a newspaper article)	Race relations in the USA Today	Word groups: race + racism, economic life (ws 1.1); portmanteau words (1.3); prepositions: over, beyond, above, across (1.4);	– –	Various excerpts from *Great Documents in Black American History* (2.3 + 2.4)	Word game (1.2); writing a research paper (3.3 + 3.4)

Title	Topic	Language	Grammar	Literature	Varia
		analysis of style, register, and speech level of M. L. King's *Letter from Birmingham Jail*	– –	– –	– –
14: June 2003: Way in the Middle of the Air (Excerpt from short story)	Future of race relations in the USA	English slang and speech levels (ws 1.1); causatives (1.2)	– –	– –	Cartoon (1.2); verbalizing photos (pp. 131 + 132)
15: Two Examples of Black American Verse	Depiction of race relations in Black American Poetry	Poetical language: figures of speech (Introducing the Topic; 5.7; 5.8)	– –	Analysing poetry: content + form (meter, rhythm, rhyme, language (5.); The sonnet (6.)	– –
16: Applicant (Sketch)	Individual suppressed by society	Wordgame: "Teekessel" Enrich your word power: show business	– –	Dramatic sketch	Phonetic exercise
17: Up im Arms over Crime (Magazine excerpts)	Crime and Self-defence in the USA	– –	Indirect Speech (ws 8)	Comic strips (8)	Crime puzzles (9.1 + 9.2); "Right to own guns" (6.1); "Death penalty" (7)

Title	Topic	Language	Grammar	Literature	Varia
18: The Seventh Victim (Excerpt from short story)	Channelling of aggression	Synonyms (ws 1.1); etymologies (1.2); abbreviations and short forms (1.3)	--	--	Hunt for hidden howlers (2.3)
19: A Message from the Falklands (Excerpts from letters)	The Falklands War – an anachronistic colonial war.	Word groups: "military"-"war" (1.1); "fill-in-the-gaps"-exercise (1.2); using annotations to write a story (1.4); analysing text type (2.8)	--	--	Interpreting a cartoon (3.2); guessing game (1.3); writing a private letter (3.3); drafting a speech (3.4)
20: The War of the Worlds (Excerpt from a radio play)	Alien invasion	Verbs + two prepositions and their synonyms (ws 1.); same spelling-different pronunciation (2.)	--	Analysis of radio play	--
21: Some Poems on War and Death	The experience of war. Its senselessness and its impact on Man and Nature	The language of poetry (2.3 + 2.4)	--	Poetry analysis: figures of speach, the relation between form and content (2.); interpretation of Ray Bradbury's *There Will Come Soft Rains* (3.2)	Modern cosmologies (3.1)

Title	Topic	Language	Grammar	Literature	Varia
22: Hiroshima (Excerpt from an account)	The destruction of Hiroshima by the atomic bomb	English terms of the German verb "machen" (1.1 + 1.3); collocations of "to make" and "to do" (1.3 + 1.4)	Simple form v. progressive form (teacher's book)	– –	Word game (1.6); analysis of an account (2.2); writing an account (4.1 + 4.2)
23: That only a Mother (Excerpt from a short story)	Nuclear War	Word families: nation, tension, family, memory (1.1); words with mute letters (1.2); paraphrases and synonyms (1.3); expressions with "nose" (1.5); analysis of figurative language (1.4)	– –	– –	Photo (p. 203); guessing game (3.6)

II SOLUTIONS AND ANSWERS

1 SHOULD WOMEN FIGHT IN WAR?

Introducing the Topic

1./2. The two short comic strips show the traditional roles that Western civilization until recently attributed to men and women:
men are the breadwinners, women – when married – take care of household and family and therefore quite automatically accept all tasks that are connected with them (e.g., dressing the children). Unmarried women (1st comic strip) normally have full-time jobs but they are rarely in top positions. The reason for this is – according to generally accepted opinion – women's lack of interest in a career. They are more interested in getting married. ("He's single.")
On the other hand, the second comic strip hints that women are no longer willing to accept their traditional role as if it were a law of nature. Today they are emancipated to such a degree that they expect men to help in household and family affairs.

4. He probably grew up in a family in which there was such a traditional division of labour. In other words, the traditional image of a man's and a woman's roles in Western society was handed down to him by his parents and he had internalized it.

5. She is tired of his permanent nagging in situations like that depicted in the comic strip. Instead of helping his wife dress the children, which would allow them to get ready in time, he prefers sitting in the car blowing the horn impatiently. Therefore she decides to teach him a lesson by taking over his role, thus demonstrating the absurdity of his behaviour.

7. Surely all the aspects mentioned (a–d) have contributed to the development of sex roles in the history of mankind. Thus, differences in natural strength and aggression between man and woman, and the fact that women bear the children, made it necessary for primitive societies to divide labour: men went hunting to provide the family with food, and women looked after the progeny. The importance of *his* task automatically gave man a *superior status* which he internalized and handed on to future generations. Moreover his *superior physical strength* made it possible for him to force his will upon the woman, consider her an object for the satisfaction of his sexual needs, and regard her as part of his personal property (male chauvinism). Little wonder that all religions (they are founded by men!) mirror this superiority of man over woman: Mary is God's *tool,* Jesus the *Saviour* of mankind. God himself is a male. It is true that Jesus treats women humanely, but they do not play an

important part in his church: his disciples are men; his church is governed and administered by men; priests are not allowed to get married; women have long been regarded as the embodiment of sin, lust and evil (Eve!). We can therefore say that religions have definitely helped affirm the image of the superiority of man and of the woman's role as man's tool, necessary to him for biological reasons.

Profound social, political and economic changes in the last two centuries (development of capitalism and of communism, growth of technology and modern industry, two world wars, etc.) have, of course, radically changed most of the traditional foundations of sex roles. On the other hand the biological difference has remained, thus making a complete exchange of sex roles impossible.

8. The picture symbolises the central topics of the book: Man and Mate thrown into the universe, having made their habitat in one of the billions of galaxies, walking hand in hand through life. But separation and hostility are already lurking: though holding each other's hands the two humans are looking (and walking?) in different directions: a symbol of discord and antagonism.

WORKSHEET

1.1 **Armed forces** (= Streitkräfte)

1. *Land* (ground) *forces* (= Landstreitkräfte)
   a) **Arms** (Waffengattungen): infantry, infantrymen; artillery; armored forces (= Panzereinheiten)
   b) **Formations and units** (= Gliederungen und Verbände)
   army; combat unit (Kampfeinheit); platoon (= Zug)
2. *Air forces* (= Luftstreitkräfte)
   a) **Arms:** – –
   b) **Formations and units:** air-crew (= Flugzeugbesatzung); pilots (= Flugzeugführer)
3. *Naval forces* (= Seestreitkräfte)
   a) **Arms:** – –
   b) **Formations and units:** ship's crew (= Schiffsbesatzung)

Military equipment: combat aircraft (= Kampfflugzeug); combat ship (= Kampfschiff); combat plane (= Kampfflugzeug); destroyer (= Zerstörer)

1.2 *Collocations:* to serve aboard/on combat ships; to endanger (the lives of) the whole unit; to weaken (our/the) armed forces; to stay in the armed forces; to improve (the quality of) the force; to assign (women) to combat units; to build a winning army; to serve on aircraft; to serve in combat planes; to keep (women) out of combat units; to put (women) in combat units; to become a fighter pilot/a destroyer captain/a platoon leader; to use (women) in combat units

1.3 a) support . . . appointment
b) restraints/limits
c) shortcomings . . . parts . . . defence
d) copy . . . emotional shock
e) consider all aspects of the issue

1.4.1 . . . is likely to happen/is likely to take place

1.4.2 Some American and English idioms:

to beat about the bush	to delay talking about or considering the most important point or part of a discussion, subject, etc.
to be not all there	to be lacking common sense
to burn the midnight oil	to work until late at night
to come to grief	to fail
to cost a mint	to be very expensive
to cut a figure	to make a good impression on s.b.
to drop a brick	to make a mistake, esp. to do or say s. th. wrong or unsuitable in a particular situation
to face the music	to face the difficulties arising from s.th. one has done
to pay on the nail	to pay in cash, to pay right away
to rain cats and dogs	to rain very heavily
to roll in money	to be very rich
to spill the beans	to let slip s.th. that is secret
to tell s.o. straight from the shoulder	to tell s.o. directly; with force and complete honesty

1.4.3 An idiom's meaning is mostly difficult to understand because "it is a fixed group of words with a special different meaning from the meanings of the separate words" *(Longman's Dictionary of English Idioms).* So the above-mentioned idiom "to spill the beans" has nothing to do with beans.

1.4.4 An idiom consists of a *fixed* group of words that are *metaphorical* rather than *literal.* Because an idiom is metaphorical one cannot usually discover its meaning by looking up the individual words in an ordinary dictionary. Because it is fixed or invariable it *cannot be changed* or *varied* in the way literal expressions can normally be varied, i.e. 1) a *substitution* of words that are close in meaning is hardly ever possible:
"the man gave up the ghost" (= died) cannot be changed into "the man gave up the apparition", nor into "the man released the ghost", nor into "the man gave him up"; 2) certain grammatical operations like the formation of the passive or the change of singular into plural are impossible. It would

sound quite wrong to say: "at 3 o'clock the ghost was given up by the man" or "the men gave up the ghosts." (*Longman Dictionary of English Idioms,* p. VIII. For further details cf. *op. cit.*)

1.4.5 a) an act or event that may seem unimportant but is considered to be the first stage of a change that might have more serious or harmful consequences. (Anfang vom Ende)

b) all of them have the same characteristics, e.g. the same faults. (= aus dem gleichen Holz geschnitzt sein)

c) to let s.o. or s.th. get out of a difficult situation; here: to allow the universities to escape financial cuts. (ungeschoren davonkommen lassen)

d) to treat s.b. gently or with (too) much caution (= mit Samthandschuhen anfassen)

e) to block back = to impede, to obstruct
to let others carry the ball = to allow others to be active, to take the offensive
here: to play his familiar role of impeding the course of certain new developments in the political arena while (at the same time) allowing others to take the offensive (= seine vertraute Rolle des Bremsers zu spielen, während er gleichzeitig zuläßt, daß andere offensiv/aktiv werden).

f) to reduce the speed at which s.th. is done. Here: Japan reduced the speed at which its economy was growing (die Bremsen anziehen).

g) humorous version of the idiom "to hit the nail on the head" (= to say s. th. that exactly describes a situation or explains the cause of a difficulty, etc.) (den Nagel auf den Kopf treffen).

h) to become successful through one's own efforts, without help from other people and in spite of disadvantages. (= aus eigener Kraft im Leben vorankommen)

1.4.6

to lose face	to lose the respect or good opinion of others
to put one's foot in one's mouth	to do or say s.th., unintentionally, that distresses or offends another person
to give s.o. a lot of lip	to talk to s.b. in an impertinent way
to lend s.o. a hand	to help s.o. do s.th.
to tell s.o. straight from the shoulder	to tell directly; with force and complete honesty
to be afoot	to be going on
with jaundiced eye	to look at s.o. in a sceptical way
to be out of one's skull	to be crazy, to be out of one's mind
s.o.'s nerves are on edge	to be very nervous
to be up to one's elbows in work	having a great deal of work to do or

	having more work than one can handle
to take a hand	here: to become concerned in, to get involved in
to foot it out of	to depart (in a hurry) from
to seethe with bile	to be furious; to fume, boil with rage
to have gall	to have the nerve
to be the heart of the matter	to be the essence of s.th.
to speak with forked tongue	to say the opposite of what one really means
to palm a thing (off) on a person	to foist/fob s.th. off on s.b.; here: to put s.th. into s.o.'s pocket without his noticing
to make s.o.'s scalp crawl	to cause s.o. to feel uneasy and fearful
to give s.o. the stony eye	to stare at s.o. unforgivingly
to have s.o. knee-capped	to hurt s.o. seriously
to give s.o. a head start	to grant s.o. an advantage over other people; here: to allow s.o. to leave first
to take it on the chin	to assume full reponsibility for s.th.
to have a heart	to feel pity for; to be kind, sympathetic
the scales have fallen from s.o.'s eyes	someone who has previously been deceived is suddenly able to realize the truth about s.th. or s.o.
to be head heels with joy	to be overjoyed with (all of a sudden); to be utterly delighted at (all of a sudden)

Translation

Cluckhorn ist ein mieser Bursche

Der Chef kam niedergeschlagen herein und sagte: „Ich habe das Gesicht verloren" („Ich habe mich blamiert"). „Wie das?" (fragte ich). „Bei der Aufsichtsratssitzung heute morgen habe ich mir wohl den Mund verbrannt." „Machen Sie sich nichts daraus. Es gibt Schlimmeres." „Ich wüßte nicht was."
„Nehmen wir mal an, Sie wären nur ein Handlanger und nicht der Chef. Jeder würde sagen: Handlanger verliert das Gesicht, indem er sich den Mund verbrennt." „Wollen Sie mich aufziehen?" „Um Gottes willen. Sehe ich so aus wie einer, der seinem Chef gegenüber eine kesse Lippe riskiert? Ich versuche doch nur, Ihnen wieder auf die Beine zu helfen. Warum sagen Sie mir eigentlich nicht frisch von der Leber weg, was und wieviel hier außer Lot ist." Er starrte mich mit skeptischem Blick an. „Haben Sie einen über den Schädel gekriegt? Bei uns hier ist ein Lot genausoviel wie überall sonst: 17 Gramm." Ich sah, daß er am Rand eines Nervenzu-

sammenbruchs stand: ja eigentlich hatte er schon mit einem Fuß den Rand überschritten. „Ich bin nicht hergekommen, um mir Ihr freches Mundwerk anzuhören", sagte er. „Sie sind doch hier angestellt, um verloren gegangenes Ansehen wieder herzustellen, oder etwa nicht? Und wenn ja, warum stecken Sie denn dann nicht schon längst bis über die Ohren in der Arbeit?"

Ich wußte, daß er mich auf die Probe stellte. Ich goß ihm drei Strich Bourbon aus dem Vorrat in meinem nierenförmigen Schreibtisch ein und sagte: „Haben Sie genug Rückgrat, um zu ertragen, was ich Ihnen sagen muß, oder sind Sie zu schwach in den Knieen, der Angelegenheit ins Auge zu sehen?"

„Sie sind recht naseweis, nicht wahr?" knurrte er. „Sicher bin ich das. Deshalb unternahm ich auch etwas, als ich Cluckhorn auf flinken Füßen aus dem Vorstandszimmer tänzeln sah. Ich sah, daß er vor Wut schäumte." „Cluckhorn schäumt immer vor Wut", sagte der Chef. „Er produziert angeblich 12 Liter Galle pro Tag." „Was viel schlimmer ist, er hätte gern Ihre Stelle." „Meine Stelle? Hat er wirklich die Stirn?" „Ja, seine Unverfrorenheit übersteigt sogar seine Übellaunigkeit", sagte ich. „Ich war heimlich, still und leise auf der medizinischen Abteilung – einfach um ein bißchen diskret herumzuschnüffeln – und habe seine Personalakte in Augenschein genommen. Er produziert (übrigens) 35 Liter Galle pro Tag." „Das ist ja haarsträubend", sagte der Chef. „Jedenfalls bemerkte ich etwas Sperriges in seiner Tasche. ‚Da liegt der Hund begraben', sagte ich zu mir selbst. Und zu Cluckhorn sagte ich: ‚Haben Sie im Vorstandszimmer ein Geschenk bekommen, Cluckhorn?'" „War seine Antwort doppelzüngig?" „Nein, das gerade nicht. Er zog den Gegenstand aus seiner Tasche und sagte: ‚Nein, nein, das ist kein Geschenk vom Vorstand. Sehen Sie selbst, es ist nur eine alte getragene Socke, die mir mein großer Bruder heute morgen beim Weggehen in die Tasche bugsierte.'" „Er hat sich mit einer gebrauchten Socke in der Tasche aus dem Vorstandszimmer geschlichen? Menschen von solchem Schlag verursachen mir eine Gänsehaut", sagte der Chef. Ich warf dem Chef einen eisigen Blick zu. „So", sagte ich zu Cluckhorn, „ich sehe, Sie haben eine getragene Socke, aber wie kommt es, daß Sie sich den Mund verbrannt haben?" „Und wie hat er darauf reagiert?" „Indem er mich beiseite drängte, mir drohte, er würde mir einen Knieschuß verpassen lassen, wenn ich ihn nicht voran gehen ließe, und sich blitzschnell die Treppe hinunter davonmachte." Der Chef starrte mich wütend an. „Cluckhorn ist ein mieser Bursche! Und", sagte der Chef, „da jemand dafür geradestehen muß, sind Sie entlassen." Er eilte zur Tür. „Wenn Sie ein Herz hätten", sagte ich, „würden Sie mir zumindest (noch) die Hand schütteln." „Ich habe keine Zeit für Gefühle. Ich komme sowieso schon zu spät zur Vorstandssitzung", sagte er. „Etwas habe ich Ihnen noch nicht erzählt", sagte ich. „Was denn?" „Mir sind die Augen aufgegangen, Herr Cluckhorn." Er drehte sich um und starrte mich an. Ich langte an seine Nase, zog kräftig – und hielt das Gesicht des Chefs in der Hand. „Der Chef wird das bestimmt brauchen können", sagte ich, „und er wird auch sicherlich nicht vor Freude an die Decke springen, wenn er hört, daß Sie mit seinem Gesicht auf und davon sind, als er sich heute morgen den Mund verbrannte und das Gesicht verlor."

Cluckhorn prallte in plötzlicher Erkenntnis zurück. „Aber, aber Sie sind ja gar nicht noch so ein unfähiger Firmenbürokrat", keuchte er. „Sie sind, Sie sind –." „Richtig, ich bin Privatdetektiv", seufzte ich, indem ich in mein Humphrey-Bogart-Lispeln verfiel.

1.4.7 a) **News from the Head of the Government**

Dear Gisela,

Thank you for your honest letter concerning "our smiling" Helmut. I immediately took a liking to you because you – just like me – must have been given "F's" in your English classes at school. In fact, I am in good company with you and your Bavarian Minister President, who – in the presence of our Eastern brothers and sisters from Leipzig – lately called a spade a spade and literally told his audience: "I think it is quite a matter of course that I should be here. Why shouldn't I pay you a visit as Head of a neighbouring state?" But notwithstanding my liking for you I must tell you plainly that I don't feel crazy about the way you make fun of one of our most important statesmen. After all, he hasn't deserved such bad treatment, in particular when you consider the stony and thorny road of his career. For instance, remember how Helmut Schmidt [the older Helmut] used to pin him down. And now we can be very, very proud of him! With his policy of "keep smiling" he has had a greater impact on people than those political figures who have forgotten how to laugh – people like the majority of the Greens and the Social Democrats.

You should rather note what the afore-mentioned famous Bavarian statesman said out of respect and love for Helmut Kohl: (I give its gist) "The Chancellor makes many ordinary German people feel and believe that they too could easily be Chancellor." Well, isn't that something? Have you ever figured out why he is so popular – not only at home but also abroad? Why else should almost 50 percent of the German voters elect him and put their trust in him? Have you any other explanation than his absolute superiority in politics? How can you dare, dear Gisela, make fun of our Chancellor in such an impertinent way? Your letter really goes too far. I tell you truly: You really go too far.

Yours sincerely,

Peter, c/o London

b) **Much Too Fat**

Dear Peter,

Excuse me if I gave you the false impression that I wanted to make fun of "our smiling Helmut". The opposite is true. He has given up laughing for quite a while and I'm really worried about his health. I'm not revealing a state secret (the Chancellor himself is aware of it and takes it seriously): he is too fat. This is definitely unhealthy – just remember the decline of the Roman Empire. It is hard to believe that such a tall man should have problems with his ideal weight. In general, people think that it is short men who put on weight too fast. But that is what I call poetic justice. Anyhow, he is showing a great sense of responsibility in acknowledging what the problem is, and in drawing the right conclusions: he took off for Austria – expressly for the purpose of losing fourteen pounds in a fortnight. Imagine that! Influential dieticians from Atkins through Brigitte to Koehnlechner were dumbfounded. Maybe the Chancellor has lately been somewhat negligent in determining the general guidelines of his policies – but whenever it is really necessary we can surely rely on him. His old trousers now fit him again. This superior attitude should be exemplary for the other members of the German Federal Lower House. While the latter keep demanding higher salaries at the expense of the German tax payer, one of our most influential statesmen has voluntarily reduced his daily consumption of calories. [Note: the pun on "Diäten" and "Kalorien" cannot be reproduced in English!] That's not an easy thing to do. Small wonder that he is a little irritable with this strain. But be assured: he is indeed a shining example for everyone in our country with weight problems. Elisabeth Noelle-Neumann, who works for the Chancellor as a political adviser, has uncovered an alarming fact: one out of three Germans, if not two out of three, is much too fat. So I warn you against eating too many apple-pies with whipped cream.

Yours truly,

Gisela

2.1.1 1) c (this statement is not necessarily in complete agreement with the text but certainly comes closer to it than the other two. The American all-volunteer forces do not need women to serve in *combat units,* but they require an increasing number of woman soldiers to keep them in existence.) 2) c; 3) b; 4) c; 5) a; 6) c

2.2.1 "War is *hell*" (metaphor); "heads are blown off, arms and legs are maimed, suffering is so intolerable" (drastic description: climax); "but do we want . . . to suffer it, too? (rhetorical question); ". . . the Army *has* women who . . . endure *three days* or *three weeks* under field conditions, *but* . . . I have *never* known 10 women whom I thought could endure *three months* . . . (antithesis, contrast); "it's pretty plain that God intended . . ." (assumptive phrase: who knows whether God intended men to be protectors in modern society, when any pregnant woman using a pistol can kill the strongest man?)

2.2.2 She strikes an emotional tone to support her arguments and persuade the readers of her opinion. She is likely to feel instinctively that some of her arguments are based on assumptions, not on proven facts, and therefore lack persuasive power.

2.2.3 Mrs Holm's diction is precise, concrete, and sober. She refers to facts, not to claims. She argues carefully, avoiding premature conclusions: "The bottom line is obviously infantry . . . We just have to wait to see what they find out . . . The Army may find I'm wrong on that . . ." She doesn't arouse an emotional response in the reader: "I think that the armed forces ought to find out what the limitations really are . . ."; "It might, it might not. If it lowers combat efficiency, then we have no choice but exclude them . . .", etc.

3.2 The students should discuss whether it is just, desirable, reasonable, and practicable to conscript women. Service of any kind would certainly satisfy the demand for justice. Whether it would be reasonable for women to spend one or two years of their lives in military or similar services, instead of spending the time on education, career, or personal happiness, is open to question. In the end, conscripting women to serve in public utilities and facilities might be doomed to failure because there may well not be enough work for young women who lack both training and experience. It's already difficult to find useful work for conscientious objectors.

3.3 The second part of this is certainly doubtful. Modern society provides sufficient technical means for women to protect themselves. Moreover, all citizens in a civilized country are protected by law. Finally, women today can co-determine whether to bear children or not. Thus, General Hoisington's remark is rather outdated.

3.4 *Pro conscription:* a) more appropriate to democracy, because it makes defence the task of all citizens and is controlled by democratically elected politicians; b) conscripted soldiers are cheaper for the tax payer; c) conscripts come from all social classes, i.e. a conscripted army may have a class-levelling effect; d) conscripts, in general, are better educated than professional soldiers.

Pro professional armed forces: a) professional soldiers get a more extended and therefore better training. This is of great advantage because modern military equipment is very sophisticated; b) professionals stay in the armed forces for longer periods of time than conscripts and are therefore more experienced; professionals can be expected to undergo tougher physical training, which results in more efficient troops; d) professionals, in general, are more highly motivated: it's their job.

4.1.1./2 The cartoon shows a male and a female soldier stiffly marching towards each other. Their faces are businesslike and there is no hint as to whether they know each other. They suddenly stop and salute, holding their hands to their caps and standing to attention. So far there hasn't been anything unusual about the two. But then – taking the onlooker by surprise – they embrace and kiss.

The message: The cartoonist certainly wants to ridicule the military forms soldiers must observe. The cartoon's effect results from the exaggerated depiction of the couple's behaviour: the two have internalized military drill to such a degree that they observe military forms (and salute!) when they meet. They do not even give up their robot-like stiffness while kissing.

However, the artist may have also intended to make fun of the military forces as a place where the sexes meet "to make love, not war". Since women were admitted to the military forces, the latter have perhaps lost their function of simply training young men to be good soldiers and have degenerated into a kind of marriage bureau. Interpreted in such a way the cartoon may also represent an indirect appeal to the public to stop the assignment of women to the military forces.

4.1.3 Some suggestions: The School of Love
Beware of the Forces!
Drill and Thrill
Ready, Steady, Go
Love in the Forces
Getting Married – Step by Step

4.2 See: Introducing the Topic, assignment 7.

4.3 The student doing this task should find that 1) (Puritan) religion only tolerates sex between married people; 2) the roles of man and woman in Puritan society are clearly defined by the Bible: the man is the head of the family and claims the respect and absolute loyalty of his wife. He, in turn, is expected to be the breadwinner and loyal husband to his wife throughout his life. The woman's role is defined as mother, housewife, and spouse who has to be at her husband's disposal but is not expected to have her own sexual needs; 3) men and women who do not come up to the expectations linked to these roles for whatever reason, are cruelly punished: put in the pillory and forced to accept the role of the social outcast. Thus Hester Prynne, who – during the two-year absence of her husband Roger Chillingworth – falls in love with Arthur Dimmesdale, a young Puritan minister, and gives birth to his child, is sentenced to wear – for the rest of her life – the red letter A (= adulteress) upon her bosom; 4) Hester Prynne, who at first accepts the role of the outcast as a just punishment for her sin, step by step recognizes the degrading and inhuman character of the Puritan laws: in other words, she is emancipated by her terrible experience. Her emancipation becomes obvious when she proposes to Arthur Dimmesdale that they shall flee to Europe: she has freed herself from the role she is expected to play in Puritan society; 5) Arthur Dimmesdale is not emancipated. He continues to regard Puritan laws as given by God. To him, Hester's suggestion is a temptation of the devil which he has to reject. Instead, he makes a public confession in the pillory, thus accepting the code of the Puritan society; 6) the author shows that the strict application of Puritan laws has a paradoxical effect. Forcing a moral code upon men and women does not lead to a genuinely moral society but to fear and hypocrisy (Dimmesdale), misery and shame (Hester), and moral degradation, hatred, and vindictiveness (Chillingworth).

2 FACIAL JUSTICE

1. The common subject is the relationship between the sexes. Whereas, e.g., *The Perfect Woman* shows a retrogression, *Facial Justice* drives the question of emancipation and equality of the sexes 'ad absurdum'.
2. The beginning of the Greek alphabet is 'alpha, beta, gamma'. 'Beta' holds the middle position, and 'betafy' is to signify that in the question of beautification of the faces a middle position is to be chosen too: the average, mediocre not-too-pretty and not-too-bad looking face of the vast majority.
3. To make them marry: thus, to reduce them to the 'common' level.
4. A case for discussion. Are women weaker than men?
5. The upheaval and unfavourable conditions necessary for such a change and revolution do not come through evolution but by force, i.e. by war. Cf. *Brave New World, 1984!*
6.

Western Democracies:	equality in face of the law, equality of opportunity
Communism:	equality in material conditions (cf. Mao's China: near-equal wages, housing, dresses, etc.)
Brave New World:	equality in happiness, biologically achieved, "conditioned" (from the "inside")
1984:	(apparent) equality in thought and feeling, love and hate, physical conditions, achieved by brainwashing (from the "outside"). (N. B. the role of 'party members', however)

   Origin of the idea of equality: Greek thought: Stoa philosophers: all human beings are endowed with reason; Christianity: equality in the face of God; Age of Enlightenment: equality = natural right; American Revolution: "all men are created equal" + "pursuit of happiness"; French Revolution: Jacobin idea of "égalité des jouissances."
7. An elderly woman as dictator is a rare if not unique example in utopian literature and open to interpretation: envious old woman? wise old woman? mother-figure who knows what's good for her children?

3 FEAR OF FLYING

Introducing the Topic

1. The cartoonist depicts a woman imprisoned in a cage and a man held on a leash by the woman. The woman's imprisonment represents her restriction to the household. He, on the other hand, has lost his freedom, too: a ring has been put through his nose, reminding the onlooker of a wild animal which has been tamed and is now controlled by its master.
2. They are married and both of them claim the right of property over their partner. Moreover, society expects her to stay at home while he goes out and provides her with the necessary means.
3. Both hate the situation, and love has long passed away. Man and woman face each other with hostility. Thus their relationship may symbolise the eternal fight between the sexes.
4. *Summary:* In his cartoon James Thurber represents a couple in a situation of mutual imprisonment. The woman behind the bars, which symbolise her restriction to the house, holds her husband on a leash fixed to his nose: symbol of her control over him. The hostile expression on their faces shows that both hate the situation, which has been caused by the rigidity of sex roles in our society.

   Comment: Thurber drew this cartoon in the late thirties or early forties. It therefore mirrors the social relationship between man and woman of *our days* only fragmentarily. No more is today's woman forced by society to stay at home. No more is it only the man who is the breadwinner of the family. However, the mutual imprisonment, the fight between the sexes, continues because *psychological* conditions have not changed, may never change. Today, partners still claim their right of property over each other. Moreover, love by itself binds man and woman together because love involves responsibility, loyalty, and the restriction of independence.

WORKSHEET

1.1 a) unable to be quiet/never at peace – – menace/danger
b) finally occupy/take over completely
c) a person having no success/a person who does not perform what is normal, expected
d) vigour/power/energy necessary to enjoy life, to be successful in life

1.2.1 colossal, enormous, extreme, very great, huge, immense, very large, terrific.

1.2.2 big, enormous, crushing, gigantic, great, huge, important, overwhelming, tremendous, vast.

1.2.3 a) All rooms in the house were in *dreadful* disorder

b) King Kong ist a *giant* ape-like monster.

c) The Aga Khan's wife wore a necklace of *dazzling* diamonds.

d) Londoners complain more and more about the *sky-rocketing* prices to be paid for owner-occupied flats.

e) The Schaubühne in Berlin has been the subject of lively debate since Peter Stein's *impressive* production of Ibsen's Peer Gynt in May 1971.

1.4 a)

SUPER WORD CIRCLE

The Wedding Party

AISLE
ATTENDANT
BEST MAN
BRIDE
BRIDESMAID
BROTHER
COUSIN
FAMILY
FLOWER GIRL
FRIEND
GROOM
MAID-OF-HONOR
MATRON-OF-HONOR
NEPHEW
NIECE
PAGE
PHOTO
RELATIVE
RING BEARER
SISTER
USHER

	1	2	3	4	5	6	7	8	9	10	11	12	13
1	R	I	N	G	B	E	A	R	E	R	A	M	T
2	E	O	N	I	C	B	E	S	T	M	A	N	B
3	L	F	N	I	R	E	G	N	M	I	L	R	L
4	A	R	B	O	C	N	A	O	D	T	I	U	A
5	T	I	I	E	H	D	P	O	U	D	S	S	O
6	I	E	I	G	N	F	F	N	E	S	A	H	R
7	V	N	N	E	R	H	O	S	I	S	T	E	R
8	E	D	T	E	O	E	M	N	F	S	H	R	E
9	M	T	B	N	P	A	W	A	O	T	U	L	I
10	A	O	O	R	I	H	M	O	O	R	S	O	E
11	E	R	O	D	I	I	E	R	L	I	T	I	C
12	A	N	L	R	L	D	B	W	A	F	E	A	O
13	O	B	F	Y	G	N	E	O	T	O	H	P	M

1.4 b) *A Wedding Ceremony*

Last year we were invited to my *sister's* wedding. The wedding ceremony took place in the Holy Trinity Church in Heidelberg. It was 10'clock sharp when the *bride* and the *groom* proceeded to the altar very slowly, very devoutly, like a queen and a king. The *aisle* was their way to paradise. To the left of the groom the *best man,* my *cousin* George, strutted along; one step behind my sister the *bridesmaid* tripped daintily. She was my *brother's friend* Jean, a very pretty girl. My whole *family* and our new *relatives* were standing in the first two rows of pews. In front of my sister some *flower girls* were strewing rose blossoms on the floor. I didn't know the girls but I was later told they were the groom's *nieces.* His *nephew,* a boy about ten years old, was the *page,* who together with my youngest sister – was carrying the train. When the bride and the groom arrived at the altar the *maid-of-honor* and the *matron-of-honor* were already awaiting them. The couple looked so happy. The *ring-bearer* handed over the rings to the groom. My mother started sobbing when the minister addressed my sister to ask her whether she would love and honour her husband. After the marriage sermon had been given and kisses exchanged, the two left the church with my sister beaming with happiness.

Outside a carriage was waiting. Before an *attendant* helped the married couple in, my father urged them to pose for the wedding *photo.* Then Doreen and Tom said good-bye, and off they went to the railway station to catch the train to Venice where they were going to spend their honeymoon. The wedding party also left quickly because it started drizzling. When I turned my head for a last glance at the church, I caught a glimpse of the *usher* who was just getting into his car with a contented smile on his face: obviously my father had given him a large tip.

2.1 a) correct; b) wrong: she is afraid of having to bear the responsibility for a child and of losing her independence; c) correct; d) wrong: she is in a confused state of mind. On the one hand she knows that having a baby means losing her indepencence, possibly giving up writing. On the other hand, she doesn't want to be an "intellectual nun", i.e. to be a woman who abstains from love and motherhood because of her career. Only the latter would mean *complete* independence from family restrictions; e) correct; f) wrong: she doesn't feel a hostage of anything. She simply *wonders* (she uses the word "maybe") whether she is a hostage of her fears; g) more wrong than right: firstly, it's wrong to say she doesn't want a baby. She *hesitates* over having a baby. Secondly, the argument (his baby!) is one reason for her hesitation, but more important is her fear of losing her independence (see b); h) wrong: she didn't write a book *on* poetry but a book *of* poetry, which did take her six years.

Arrangement in a logical order (for writing a summary)

1:a; 2:c; 3:b (corrected!); 4:d (corrected!); 5:e;
Statements f, g, h are unnecessary for the summary because in part they repeat (g) what has already been said in point d (corrected!) or they are of less importance (f and h).

3.1 Certainly. It is true that the pressure of society on women to have children, and to give up a career in favour of family life, has somewhat decreased during the past few years (see *USA women: They want self-fulfillment* below). But Isidora's problem is not only pressure from outside. She actually wants a child but she also knows the possible disadvantages for her career of having a child. That's the real dilemma she is in. For the women of the 1980's this is still an unsolved problem as the poll below seems to show: ". . . 63% of women want a career with marriage and family . . ." But ". . . a majority of women (80%) . . . now say that a happy marriage does not necessarily need children." (Is this a recognition that still today having both career and children is impossible?)
The main difficulty working mothers have to overcome is to find somebody to care for the child(ren) during their absence from home. Moreover, mothers often feel miserable and guilty when they themselves cannot devote enough time to the education of their children. So a large number of so-called career women decide to abandon their plans for marriage and motherhood.

USA women: They want self-fulfillment

By Michelle Healy
USA TODAY

A loving husband is no longer as important as self-fulfillment to USA woman, a new nationwide poll shows.
The emphasis on career and interests outside the family is a recurring theme in the 1985 Virginia Slims American Women's Opinion Poll, released Sunday. Interviews with 3,000 women and a control group of 1,000 men showed marriage and kids are not enough.
"Over the past 15 years, we've been seeing enormous changes in . . . what women wanted generally out of life", says Shirley Wilkins, president of The Roper Organization Inc., which conducted the poll. This is the fifth such survey. The first was taken in 1970.
Eleven years ago, 64 percent of women ranked having a loving husband as more important than self-fulfillment. Today, only 48 percent feel that way, and 72 percent of women say that marriage is not a prerequisite for happiness.
Although the infusion of women into low-level jobs has left most with the

feeling of having "just a job" instead of "a career", 85 percent get "great" or "moderate" personal satisfaction from working.

The poll also shows:

- 63 percent of women want a career with marriage and family. A decade ago only 52 percent chose both.
- 52 percent of women work full or part-time, compared with 29 percent in 1970.
- Given the choice to work outside the home or be homemaker, 51 percent would choose working, up from 35 percent in 1974.
- 57 percent of women and 50 percent of men say a marriage in which husbands and wives share responsibilities – employment, child care – is the most satisfying, up from 46 percent and 44 percent, respectively, in 1974.
- A majority of women (80 percent) and of men (76 percent) now say that a happy marriage does not necessarily need children.
- For the first time in 15 years, more women than men (73 percent vs. 69 percent) say they approve of efforts to strengthen women's status.
- 74 percent of married, employed men would feel comfortable if their wives made more money than they do, up 11 percent since 1980. Only 68 percent of employed women are comfortable making more, up from 59 percent a decade ago.

From: USA TODAY, 22 Oct. 1985

3.2 It's hard to find a solution to her dilemma in our society. Children need love and few husbands are prepared to give up their position or career in favour of their wives. Little wonder that the number of mothers who are managers, professors, or politicians is relatively small. Isidora should try to find a husband who is ready to look after the child(ren). But there is no solution to the fact that a woman often develops closer emotional ties to the father of her child(ren) than to a man with whom she has no child(ren).

3.3 They are a family apparently very much concerned to live according to how society expects them to.

3.4 "Fear of Flying" is to be understood as "fear of being emancipated", i.e. Isidora has to grapple with the fears and doubts any person faces who wants to be free of the conventions of society, but isn't sure whether he/she can stand the social pressures resulting from the attempt at emancipation.

3.5 The woman of the 1980's has certainly gained more social independence and freedom than she had in the early 1970's. It's quite normal for a woman of today to go to a bar or restaurant without being harassed, to do jobs which back in the 70's were still thought to be "jobs for men", and to co-determine whether to have any children and when. But, on the other hand, it's undoubtedly women who suffer most from unemployment because many people think that when work is short women should give up their jobs to provide work for men. In that respect, the emancipation of women has definitely experienced a setback in the 1980's.

3.6 The following figures are from 1982:
West Germany: 10.1 births per 1,000 population
East Germany: 14.4
United Kingdom: 12
France: 14
Italy: 13

Source: *Diercke Weltstatistik 84/85,* dtv/westermann, 1984

3.7 With the exception of East Germany the birthrates have continued to decrease between 1973 and 1982.
Reasons:
- Higher living standards
- Growing unemployment
- Increase in female workforce
- Rise in number of career women
- Rise in women's marriage age (better education)
- Changed attitude towards children (considered a burden rather than a blessing)
- Environmental concerns (industrialized countries using up too many natural resources; people produce waste)
- Safer contraceptives and more possibilities of using them
- Legalized abortion in most countries

3.8 *Positive consequences:*
- Less environmental pollution
- Higher quality of life
- Gradual reduction of unemployment
- Better education of students (smaller classes)
- Decline in crime rate (young people commit most crimes)

Negative Consequences:
- Slowdown of economic growth (fewer consumers)
- Temporary increase in teacher's unemployment
- Growing social and political immobility (old people are more conservative)
- Decline of new ideas and innovations in science and technology
- Increasing difficulty in providing pensioners with reasonable old age benefits

Relations with the Third World:
The decline of economic growth in industrialized countries because of the

decline in the birthrate could have a number of negative effects on Underdeveloped and Semideveloped Countries:

– Reduction in development aid would result in more hunger in UDCs and growing political tensions between Developed and Underdeveloped countries.
– Lower demand for natural resources in industrialized countries would result in diminishing living standards in semi-developed countries
– Hunger and diminishing living standards might add to the number of so-called economic refugees
– Rise of racial tensions in industrialized countries with a high percentage of immigrants from UDCs

4 a) The picture on the left mirrors the woman's traditional role of homemaker. It is she who is interested in seeing the house behind the brickwall.
Clichés: women are weak and nosey, men are strong and gentleman-like.
The picture on the right shows the very opposite: an exchange of traditional roles: she goes to work and earns the living, he stays at home and does the housework.
b) – –

Grammar: Relative Clauses

1. The text *Fear of Flying* contains 21 relative clauses. Find them and explain
   a) which of them are defining, resp. non-defining
   b) why different relative pronouns (which, who, that, what) are used
   c) why the relative pronoun is sometimes left out
   d) why no relative clause used in the text is put between commas
2. Make one sentence out of the two given by using a relative clause (defining or non-defining). Use a contact clause whenever possible.
   Insert commas where necessary.
   Ex.: My girl friend is living in Oxford. She is a typist.
   Sol.: My girl friend, who is living in Oxford, is a typist.
   a) In 1962, the Government introduced the Commonwealth Immigrants Act. The latter gave it power to restrict the number of people entering Britain from the Commonwealth.
   b) Parliament has started a new session. It is going to pass the new Bill today.
   c) In 1971, 15 was the school-leaving age. It was raised to 16 in 1972.
   d) The 900 or so magistrates courts consist of a "bench" of three lay unpaid magistrates. Their function is to ascertain the facts of a case and apply the law to them.
   e) They sold their shares last year. It was definitely a grave error.

f) These are the shares. He bought them yesterday.
g) He asked for an increase in salary last week. His boss refused it, though.
h) My wife has several friends. They are all girls from her school.
i) This is Mr Maier. His wife is American.
j) London and some other large towns have huge flocks of starlings. Especially in winter, they congregate to roost on buildings.

3. Insert the correct relative pronoun or leave it out where possible. Put the commas where necessary. (Note: Sometimes you must also insert a fitting preposition)
Heidelberg itself was dismal. A beautiful town _______ it rains ten months of the year. The sun struggles to appear for days, comes out for an hour or so, and then retreats again. And we were living in a prison of sorts. A spiritual and intellectual ghetto _______ we literally could not leave without being jailed.
I used to walk the streets of the old town alone in the rain. I spent hours wandering through department stores fingering merchandise _______ I knew I'd never buy, dreaming in crowds overhearing long conversations _______ at first I understood only snatches of. Sometimes, wandering around aimlessly, I would have the fantasy that I was the ghost of a Jew _______ had been murdered in a concentration camp on the day _______ I was born. I devised complicated plots _______ I pretended to myself were merely surrealistic tales _______ I planned to write. For the first time in my life, I became intensely interested in the history of the Jews, especially of those _______ home had been Heidelberg, and in the history of the Third Reich. I began poring over books _______ detailed the horrors of the deportations and death camps. I explored Heidelberg like a spy, finding all the landmarks of the Third Reich _______ were deliberately not mentioned in the guidebooks. I found the place where the synagogue had stood before it was burnt down. I felt like one of those fanatical Israelis _______ tracks down Nazis in Argentina and Brazil. Only I was tracking down my own past, my own Jewishness _______ I had never been able to believe before.
_______ infuriated me most, I think, was the way the Germans had changed their protective coloration, the way they talked peace and humanitarianism. It was their hypocrisy _______ I abhorred. In the three years _______ I lived in Germany I only met one man _______ admitted that he loved Hitler. He was a former Nazi and he became my friend.
After a year of hunting Nazis in Heidelberg (and taking a strange series of odd jobs, all _______ only increased my depression) Bennett and me set up house in Mark Twain village, a vast American concentration camp in the post-war section of town (a far cry from the beautiful old section near the Schloss _______ tourists see). Our neighbours were mostly army captains and their dependants _______ – with a few notable exceptions – were the most considerate people _______ I've ever lived among. It was all the more astonishing then when they announced to you that the US ought to bomb the hell out of the Viet Cong, and that soldiers were only there to do a job but not to have political opinions.

I can still close my eyes and remember the dinner hour in Mark Twain Village. The smell of TV dinners in passageways. Twenty-five-year old freckle-faced matrons from Kansas wandering about in housecoats and hair rollers, always awaiting that Cinderella evening ______ it will be worthwhile to comb out their curls. It never comes. Instead come the salesmen ______ stalk the hallways, ringing door bells, selling everything from picture encyclopedias (in simplified vocabulary) to Oriental rugs to Black Forest cuckoo clocks ______ chime perpetually. When the cuckooing itself wasn't infuriating me, the symbolism of the clocks amused me. Everyone in the army was always counting the days and minutes ______ didn't seem to pass: eight more months before you rotate, three more months before your husband goes to Vietnam, two more years before you are eligible for promotion, three more months before you can send for your wife and child . . . The cuckoos recorded every minute of every hour in that long march toward oblivion.
Adapted from: Erica Jong, *Fear of Flying.*

Solution

1. line 10: which; (13): which; (15): woman I could – who; (17): who – what – what; (18): who – what; (19): girl I might; (22): that; (29): which; (30): who; (38): who; (39): which; (40): who – who; (41): a man you; (42): that; (47): what – what
   Note: "what" in lines 8/10 have not been counted because here they introduce an indirect question rather than a relative clause.
   a) all relative clauses are *defining,* which is not surprising since the author uses a colloquial rather than a neutral speech level
   b) *who:* used for persons (subject case); *which: for things (subject and direct object case); that:* only used in defining rel. clauses; in l. 22: it simply replaces "which" (subject of rel. cl.); in 1.42: "that" ist preferred to "which" *following superlatives* or similar expressions; *what:* used as a generalising relative pronoun, instead of "anything that" or in a determinative function instead of "that which": l. 17: instead of "anything that"; l. 18: instead of "that which"; l. 47: "anything that"
   c) contact clauses: the relative pronoun can be *dropped* if it is the *direct object* of a *defining* rel. cl.
   d) all rel. cls. are defining. Only *non-def.* rel. cls. are *put* in *commas.*
2. a) which/that; b) Parliament, which has started a new session, is . . .; c) . . . age, which was raised . . .; d) whose function . . .; e) . . . the shares last year, which was . . .; f) . . . the shares he bought . . .; g) His boss refused the . . . he asked for; h) . . . several friends, all of whom are girls . . .; i) . . . Mr Maier whose wife . . .; j) . . . starlings which especially in winter, congregate . . .
3. . . . town in which; ghetto which; merchandise – –; conversations which; Jew who; day – –; plots which; tales – –; those whose; books which/that; Reich

which/that; Israelis who; Jewishness in which; what infuriated; hypocrisy – –; years – –; man who; all of which; Schloss, which; dependants who; people – –; evening for which; salesman who; clocks which/that; minutes which/that

4 PERFECT WOMAN

1.1 More examples: checkup, hangover (both in the text), upcoming (Br. use: forthcoming) negotiations, communist takeover, a program line-up, a student sitin, handouts for the history class, a terrible political setback, a funny-looking dress-up, a political showdown.

Other characteristics of the English language:

- loss of inflexions system (except for genitive)
- loss of conjugational system (except for 3rd pers. sg.)
- shortening of words in infinitive: many one-syllable words in English (German gehen – English go)
- loss of case and number of adjective: (out of) a big house, two big houses; German: ein großes Haus, zwei große Häuser
- mingling of past tense and past participle in weak verbs: loved – liebte, geliebt
- back-formation: housekeeper – to housekeep, to babysit, to typewrite, to backbite

1.2 Equality: equal, equalize, equalitarian (egalitarian), unequal

unpleasant: please, pleasure, pleasant, pleasurable (angenehm, freudig)

insufferable: suffer, sufferance, sufferer, sufferable (ertragbar)

unreconstructed: construct, reconstruct, construction, constructive, constructional (baulich, Bau-, Konstruktions-)

perceptibly: perception, perceive, perceivable, perceptiveness (Einfühlsamkeit, Scharfsinnigkeit)

perfect: to perfect, perfectible, perfection.

1.3 drink: sip – nippen, schlürfen; gulp – schlucken, würgen; sup – nippen, löffeln; tipple – zechen, picheln; guzzle – saufen (gas-guzzler!), fressen; carouse – zechen, trinken

eat: feed – füttern, ernähren; devour – verschlingen; swallow – verschlucken; gulp – würgen; dine – speisen; tuck in – "verdrücken", "reinhauen".

think: consider – nachdenken über; reflect – nachsinnen über; speculate – Vermutungen anstellen; study – studieren; brood – brüten über; contemplate – nachdenklich betrachten, überdenken.

walk: march – marschieren; step – schreiten, treten; tread – treten; pace – (ab)schreiten; trudge – stapfen, sich fortschleppen; stride – (aus)schreiten; toddle – watscheln (von kleinen Kindern, cf. toddler).

2.1.1 Primitive Woman:
bundle of neuroses (l. 12); neurotic creatures (l. 45); unreconstructed (l. 49); egoistic, spoiled, demanding care and attention, make husbands wash dishes, asking for money to buy clothes and trinkets, demanding breakfast in bed and dashing off to bridge games, equal (ll. 49–54); coarse mental fiber (l. 77); stamina (l. 81).
Modern Woman:
nice and responsive (l. 11); bustling around (l. 25); enveloping love (l. 56); finely balanced sensibilities, finest dearest qualities of femininity (l. 79); lack of stamina (l. 81);

2.1.2 – –

2.1.3 "Modern" woman is actually the type of a loving and caring (house)wife in her unequal, traditional role.
"Primitive" woman instead resembles an emancipated, equal woman of our time, yet still dependent on her husband for money, clothes etc.

2.2 Six steps: 1: "Have you noticed her reflexes?" (l. 16); 2: out of sorts (l. 20); 3: it was the right answer, but it had taken too long (l. 61); 4: something was terribly wrong (l. 65); 5: her eyes were becoming unfocused (l. 86); 6: on the way back to the factory (l. 103).

2.3 sf: android women, seffiners, Stat, speaking or listening car and garage – **technology.** Conservative: parties, slacks, bridge, preparation of breakfast, washing of dishes, work, communication via telephone, mail – **society.**

2.4 "Stat": state, God. "Seffiners": rolls, waffles. Might indicate great power of state. A new term suggesting a new society.

3.1 Because men command and master technology. This reflects the traditional view: boys play with technical things, girls with dolls. Men are technical-minded, practical-minded, women are social-minded.

3.2 It shows a conservative male stereotype of woman: loving, kissing, yes-saying, praising, caring, respecting wife, who resembles a mother ("feeding him", l. 58).

3.3 It's actually a step backwards: woman as the ultimate househould machine, symbolizing the male dream of superiority through technology.

4.1 – –

4.2 THREE PEOPLE from different parts the country passed away at the same time. They all went up to heaven and were met at the gate by St. Peter. The first person was an architect from California. "I'd like to come in, please," he told the saint.
"All in good time," replied St. Peter. "But first you have to pass one small test. You have to spell 'God'."
"Oh, that's easy", said the architect. "G-o-d."
"Very good", said St. Peter. "Come on in."

The second person to approach the gate was a rancher from Texas. "I'd sure like to enter", he said.
"All in good time", replied St. Peter. "But first you have to pass a little test. All you have to do is spell 'God'."
"Simple", said the Texan. "G-o-d."
"Very good", answered St. Peter. "You can come in."
Then the third person, an attractive businesswoman from New York, approached the saint.
"I'd like to enter, please."
"Well", said the saint, "you'll have to pass one small test –"
"Oh, come on now, Saint", said the woman. "I've had it rough all my life. Just because I'm a woman I've had to fight for every promotion I've ever gotten. I've had to take lower pay for the same jobs as my male colleagues, and I've been continually harassed at work by an MCP boss. Now are you going to give me a hard time too?"
"But it's just a little test", repeated St. Peter. "Spell 'Czechoslovakia'."

WOMEN's lib has done wonders for the guilt feelings of us American men. Recently, I had a seat on a crowded bus, and a woman was standing in front of me. I said, "Pardon me, but are you a member of women's lib?" She said, "Yes, I am." I said, "Is that the organization that wants women to stand on their own two feet?" She said, "Yes, it is." I said, "Right on!"

5 A LEGAL, MORAL, SOCIAL NIGHTMARE

WORKSHEET 1.1/2

Annotation	German	Noun	Verb	Adjective	Synonym/
nightmare	Alptraum	see annotation	– –	nightmarish	terrible
in-vitro ferti- lization	Befruchtung im Reagenzglas	see annotation	to fertilize	fertile	artificial procre-
procreation	Fortpflanzung	see annotation	to procreate	procreative	generating off-
womb	Gebärmutter, Unterleib, Schoß	see annotation	– –	– –	organ in a female
surrogate mother	Leihmutter	see annotation	to surrogate	– –	woman who 1)
cancer	Krebs	see annotation	– –	cancerous	diseased growth
to sue	jem. verklagen	– –	see annotation	– –	make a legal
seed	Spermium	see annotation	to seed	– –	1) flowering
infant	Kleinkind	see annotation	– –	infantile	child during
physician	Arzt, Chirurg	see annotation	– –	– –	doctor of medi-
dubious	zweifelhaft	dubiousness	– –	see annotation	doubtful, ques-

Paraphrase	Antonym
frightening dream; sth. dreaded; memory of a horrible experience	sweet dream, vision
ation achieved by removing an egg from a woman's ovary, placing it in a dish and adding sperm for fertilization.	– –
spring	– –
mammal in which offspring is carried and nourished while developing before birth	– –
carries the child that was produced by artificial insemination with the sperm of the husband of an infertile woman or 2) carries a testtube embryo	– –
in the cells of organs, often causing death	– –
claim against s.b.	– –
plant's element of life, from which another plant can grow 2) fertilizing sperm produced in the male reproductive organs	– –
the first few years of its life	adult
cine and surgery	– –
tionable, suspicious	positive, harmless, unsuspicious

1.3 surrogate; bearing; womb; insemination; womb; surrogacy; arrangements; pregnancies; infertile; inability; birth; maternal/motherly

1.4 to deal with; to range from . . . to; to give s.th. up; to be liable to; to die of; to ask for; to be impregnated with; to rest on; to side with; to be separated from; to have a right to; to derive from; to be an argument against; to endow s.o. with; to call upon; to fertilize with; to be implanted in; to grant rights to; to refrain from; to be limited to; to chafe at; to leave s.th. to s.o.; to screen s.o. for s.th.; to happen in; to rely on; to be proud of

1.5 by; along, on; for; for; for; of; On; along, on; – –; – –; With; for; of; in; from; with; into; – –; into; in; to; of

2. a) The basic reason, of course, is their failure to have the child they urgently want. The cause of their difficulty is often their proneness to miscarriage. Thus, a couple who are childless because of that particular problem have to undergo a combination of IVF and surrogacy to have a child of their own.

b) All these modern techniques of fertilization can be seen in two ways: they help infertile couples to fulfil their desire to have a baby, but on the other hand they turn conjugal love into a merely mechanical process, by making the creation of new life a laboratory experience. In this way, human procreation is in danger of losing its personal dimension and of becoming something akin to animal husbandry. Commercial surrogacy, in particular, emphasizes this loss of personal relationship, because it reduces the surrogate mother to a kind of machine who can be rented or bought and switched on at whim.

c) The contracts may not be legally binding because surrogacy has not yet been brought within the code of the law. Consequently, there are no legal guidelines to help resolve possible disputes.

d) There could well be a number of legal and social problems. For instance, the question could arise as to whether single men or homosexual couples could make use of surrogate mothers. Or what happens if the surrogate mother drinks or takes drugs, and the baby is mentally handicapped or otherwise damaged? What about frozen embryos if the parents die? Should they be killed or do they have a right to life?

e) – –

f) It says that any embryo is a live entity whose life is given by God and therefore has certain rights, above all the right not to be killed. However, artificial reproduction leads to the death of embryos (fertilized eggs) because only a few of them may be needed. Or they do not attach to the uterine lining and are consequently expelled from the womb. Last, but not least, the Catholic church rejects all these techniques because they represent an unacceptable interference with nature or God's will.

g) The cases of Corinne Parpalaix and Mr and Mrs Rios. Mrs Parpalaix's husband had deposited his seed in a sperm bank. After his death Mrs Parpalaix wanted to be impregnated with his seed. The sperm bank refused on the grounds that Mr Parpalaix had not decided what should be done with his seed. Mrs P. sued and the judge decided that Mr P.'s seed should be handed over to Mrs P.

Mr and Mrs Rios died in an air-crash soon after they had deposited in an Australian clinic, for later implantation, two frozen embryos created from Mrs Rios's eggs and the sperm of an unknown donor. The resulting question was: should these be destroyed or kept alive? (So far they have been kept alive in accordance with a judge's order.)

h) – –

6 PROBLEMS OF THE FAMILY TODAY

Introducing the Topic

1.1 Key words: Leaving home; free; (living) alone; fun (denied)

1.2 See text of song

1.3
a) What did the girl do one Wednesday morning?
b) Why did she leave home?
c) Why did she leave a note?
d) What did she take with her?
e) How did her mother respond to the girl's disappearance?
f) What regrets did she come out with?
g) Where was the girl two days later?
h) Who was she waiting for?
i) How did the girl feel now that she had left home?
j) What does the song say about "having fun"?

2.1

Heroin:	desired effect: euphoria ("psychological high") possible negative effects: classic addiction, physical decline, death. Withdrawal symptoms: restlessness, nausea
Other opiates:	see heroin (physical decline is less fast)
Tranquilizers:	desired effects: calming down nervous restlessness; overcoming sleeplessness possible negative effects: classic addiction, physical decline
Hallucinogens:	(Phencyclidine [PCP]; LSD; mescaline) desired effect: extension of brain activity and creation of wider spectrum of perceptions (colours, odours, sounds) possible negative effects: disturbance of behaviour and loss of contact with reality, impaired memory and perceptions, anxiety and depression.

Sedatives:	(hypnotic drugs) desired effects: reduction of tensions, inducing of sleep; euphoria possible negative effects: addiction, loss of consciousness, coma, death
Cocaine:	desired effects: euphoria; sense of power; clarity of mind possible negative effects: addiction, depression; hallucinations; nausea; sleeplessness; loss of weight. Larger doses can cause convulsions, and death from respiratory failure
Inhalants:	(gasoline; paint thinners; dry-cleaning solutions; toluene) desired effects: euphoria; excitement possible negative effects: physical damage to the brain; disturbances in heart rhythm; sudden death
Marijuana:	desired effect: euphoria possible negative effects: hallucinations; depression; extreme variability of mood; reddening of eyes; increase in the rapidity of the heart beat. Chronic use does *not* establish physical dependence; no physical discomfort upon withdrawal
Cigarettes:	desired effects: relaxation; pleasant feelings possible negative effects: addiction; cancer; high blood pressure; circulatory disease
Alcohol:	desired effects: relaxation; relief of stress; pleasant feelings; escape from reality possible negative effects: addiction, physical and social decline; death

REASONS for taking drugs: a) escape from reality and social pressures (young people; people who are socially unstable) b) increase in mental and creative abilities (intellectuals; artists) c) increase in physical endurance (people working under extreme conditions like heat, moist climate; sportsmen) d) relief of fear, hunger, pain, depression (soldiers; poor people) e) curiosity (young people)

2.2 – –

WORKSHEET

1.1 *marriage:* couple, husband, wife (divorcee, to divorce)
lineage: family, father, mother, parents
descendants: children, daughter, kids, son, boy

relatives by blood: brother, folks
relatives by marriage: parents-in-law

1.2 Some further expressions: *marriage:* bride, spouse
lineage: ancestors, forefathers, grandfather, -mother
descendants: grandchild, granddaughter, grandson
relatives by blood: aunt, nephew, niece, sister, uncle
relatives by marriage: father-in-law, mother-in-law, son-in-law, stepfather, stepmother

1.3 a) The elderly couple were glued to a settee and to each other by their former son-in-law.
b) A deed that causes feelings of loathing and offends people's ideas of what is decent.
c) Also Guilty dressed her children in the middle of the night and left home.
d) Her anger reached a point where it was impossible for her to get more furious.
e) Having reached the limits of what she was able to bear, Also Guilty lost self-control and began to act insanely when the children started a fight.

1.4.1 The suffix -ee, in general, signifies a person who receives something or to whom s.th. is done (some exceptions exist, for instance "escapee": der Ausbrecher), whereas the suffix -er/or (also -ar) describes a person who does s.th. actively.

1.4.2

	-er/or	-ee	German	
agree	agreer	– –	– –	

(see D. Hare: *A Map Of The World,* faber and faber, p. 28.)

appoint	– –	appointee	– –	Angestellter, Berufener
consign	consignor	consignee	Versender, Überweisender	Empfänger, Bezieher
contain	container	– –	Behälter	– –
deal	dealer	– –	Händler	– –
devote	– –	devotee	– –	Anhänger, Verehrer
draft	– –	draftee (US)	– –	Wehrdienst-pflichtiger, "Gezogener"
draw	drawer	drawee	Aussteller (Wechsel)	Wechselschuld-ner, "Bezoge-ner"

drive	driver	– –	Fahrer	– –
employ	employer	employee	Arbeitgeber	Arbeitnehmer, Angestellter
let (!)	lessor	lessee	Vermieter	Mieter
license	licenser	licensee	Lizenz-erteiler	Lizenznehmer
nominate	nominator	nominee	Ernenner	Ernannter
sell	seller	– –	Verkäufer	– –
supply	supplier	– –	Lieferant	– –
support	supporter	– –	Anhänger	– –
talk	talker	– –	Schwätzer	– –
train	trainer	trainee	Ausbilder	Auszubildender
vote	voter	– –	Wähler	– –

Note: This word formation is very productive. It may be that words like "suppliee", "drivee", or "votee" are already now and then in use.

1.4.3 1) A container is a large box in which goods are transported.
2) German car dealers sold more than 3 million automobiles last year.
3) Car drivers need nerves of steel during the summer, because then the motorways are terribly congested.
4) In 1983, the majority of German voters voted for the Christian Democrats.
5) Employers keep saying that employers and employees are all in the same boat.
6) A draftee has to serve 18 months in the Federal Armed Forces.
7) The abductors released the abductee after his family had paid a ransom of 2 million DM.
8) Most trainees find a job after their training.

1.4.4 The man is reading a letter: Derivatives reader
His wife is watching the children: watcher
The children are walking out of the room: walker
The woman is knitting socks: knitter
The man is speaking to his wife: speaker

1.4.5 a) drawer; drawee; Drawer b) trainees c) dealer/seller d) lessee; lessor e) containers f) addressee's g) employee h) dealers; employees

1.5 *Court proceedings:* to plead guilty to = sich schuldig bekennen
Crown Court: Staatsgericht für schwere Straftaten, Jugendgerichtssachen etc.

Prosecutor: Ankläger, Staatsanwalt
District Court: Bezirksgericht
Jury: die Geschworenen
Attorney: hier: Staatsanwalt (auch Rechtsanwalt)
Testimony: Zeugenaussage
Trial: Prozeß, Gerichtsverhandlung
In defense: zur Verteidigung
Lawyer: Rechtsanwalt

2.1/2 The impression given is that violence is a normal event between couples and within families. This impression is certainly misleading. Life in the majority of families is non-violent. Of course, quite a number of children may get spanked now and then, but this kind of violence has little to do with the cases mentioned in the headlines and news.

2.3
a) The pressures of a working life. They cause many men and women to let off steam at home.
b) The increased use of drugs (alcohol, etc.) which can trigger off aggressiveness.
c) The emancipation of women: 1) many working women expect their husbands to take over a fair share of the housework. This often causes disputes because many men do not come up to such expectations; 2) working women are financially independent and thus more prepared to seek a divorce when they feel exploited or badly treated by their husbands.
d) The increased number of women in the workforce. This leads to more contacts between men and women: "Opportunity makes the thief." Jealousy resulting from adultery may be expressed as violence.
e) The general decline of religious life and the development of what is called the "permissive society".
f) people live longer and therefore have to live longer together, which often results in monotony and alienation.

2.4 A Some positive consequences for the family and society:
a) more women (than at present) will be independent from men.
b) mutual tolerance and cooperation between man and woman may be enhanced.
c) women may draw satisfaction from their work outside the home. This may have a positive influence on family life.
d) increased family income may lead to better education of the children, and contribute to a higher degree of satisfaction.
e) a possible increase in consumption helps to keep the economy growing.
f) in many fields women do a better job than men. This may result in a rise of the quality of production. Higher productivity may also result because women's absenteeism is lower than that of men.

B Some negative consequences:

a) working women are often tired and irritable: increase in dissatisfaction and rise in divorce rate

b) lower birthrate may lead to social and economic problems in the long run: the aging of society may result in increasing difficulty in paying pensions and old age benefits; mental lethargy, lack of social progress, technological stagnation; loss of economic competitiveness

c) children may be neglected: higher rate of juvenile delinquency, increase in drug addiction

2.5 Unless natural procreation, i.e. family in general, is abolished in the future (see *MW* 2, p. 58 ff.), the nuclear family will certainly survive because in the late twentieth century the extended family lacks attraction. Most young couples want to be independent, even though the extended family offers the advantage that both man and woman can work out of house leaving the parents to look after the children. However, more and more couples will live together and have children without a certificate legalizing their union.

As far as alternatives are concerned it may be possible that living together in a so-called commune will become increasingly attractive to young couples, because this type of "family" obviously combines a fair amount of individual freedom with the distribution of tasks and responsibility among a larger number of people. However, since the various couples living together are – in general – not related by blood or by law, these social units are more likely to break down. So far most communes have suffered from instability.

2.6./7 Unlike some other newspapers, *The Sun* turns fact into sensation by a) providing information that cannot be proved: nobody can know the reason for the boy killer's escape. *The Guardian's* headline therefore dispassionately clings to the facts; b) by making use of emotive language (= playing with the feelings of the readers). Whereas *The Guardian* uses the more abstract term "escape", *The Sun* employs the Anglosaxon "broke out", which is more dynamic and concrete. *The Sun's* headline to the news item about the man who "broke into the home of his former parents-in-law" applies the emotive term "terror" to strike a sensational note and attract prospective readers; c) by using oversized type that creates an impression of special importance.

By turning facts into sensations, newspapers like *The Sun* aim at an enormous circulation and are therefore called "popular" newspapers. Others are: *The Daily Mirror* (left wing), *The Star, The Express,* and *The Daily Mail* (right wing). Newspapers like *The Guardian* (liberal) which report news in a sober, dispassionate way, are called "quality" newspapers. Others are: *The Times* (conservative), *The Daily Telegraph* (conservative)

2.8 Headlines rarely use: a) articles; b) forms of "to be" (particularly in passive sentences); c) descriptive adjectives and adverbs; d) dependent clauses (relative clauses excepted)
Suggestion: To show the students what this artificial brevity of Journalese may lead to, write the following headlines on the blackboard and get the students to work out what they mean. (The examples are taken from: Philip Howard, *The State of the Language,* English Observed, Hamish Hamilton, London 1984.)
SQUAD HELPS DOG BITE VICTIM
(dog bite victim = person bitten by a dog)
DEAD EXPECTED TO RISE
(to rise: to increase [in number]; to come to life)
MAN EATING PIRANHA MISTAKENLY SOLD AS PET FISH

ALLIES PUSH BOTTLES UP GERMANS
(push: military advance; to push up [sl.]: in den Anus stecken
to bottle up: to take in a trap)

2.9 The introductory paragraph of news frequently provides the reader with a short survey of the most important facts given in the item. In many cases it is printed in bold type.

2.10 Yes. The first paragraph of "Woman weds . . ." serves the same function.

2.11 – –

2.12 Sense unit 1: I must . . . – – I have been there. (Reference to a previous letter to the editor; Also Guilty's reason for writing the letter to Ann Landers)
Sense unit 2: A few years ago . . . – – me a divorce. (Background information)
Sense unit 3: One day . . . – – I had become. (Reasons for Also Guilty's loss of self-control; her striking her daughter)
Sense unit 4: I had never . . . – – getting it. (The impact of this experience on Also Guilty)
Sense unit 5: I am sure . . . – – because I am Also Guilty (Suggestion for reducing the problem of child abuse)

2.13 – –

3.1 Dear Also Guilty:
Thank you for reminding us once again that there are two sides to every story. Yours was an isolated incident, provoked by the piling up of stressful situations you couldn't cope with. Many acts of child abuse, however, are repeated assaults involving broken bones, concussion, and cigarette burns. Those are the ones that must be investigated and stopped. Thank you for writing. You sound like a warm-hearted person and good mother.
From: *Stars & Stripes*, Febr. 10, 1983

3.2 – –

3.3 MOTHER FOUND GUILTY OF CHILD ABUSE

Venice, Md.

Anne Cooper, 20, from Venice, Md., was sentenced yesterday to serve two months in prison for injuring her one-year old daughter Mary. The three-man, three-woman District Court jury decided that Anne Cooper was guilty of repeatedly beating her daughter so hard that the child was bruised all over her body. According to witnesses the child cried for hours almost daily.

When asked by the judge why she had treated her child so badly, the divorced woman said that she couldn't stand the girl's continual crying. "At nights I didn't get any sleep, and during the day I had a part- time job, to earn our living. In the end I was a bag of nerves."

The girl has meanwhile been taken into care for the time the convict has to serve in prison.

3.4

a) He was jealous.
b) Let's assume "Yes", he was drunk ("bar!")
c) Yes, she danced with another man.
d) He is very unstable and given to outbursts of violent temper.
e) He is an only child. Until recently he lived with his mother, who is divorced. His father is a notorious drunkard who beat his wife and son frequently.
f) Yes.
g) No, he attended school only irregularly. He has never mastered spelling, and he starts stammering when he gets nervous.
h) Yes. Her education is no better than his, but her IQ is 110, compared with the defendant's 85.

Your Honour, Jury of Weston County District Court,

The law requires you to pass a judgement on this man. He is accused of biting part of the nose off Ginger Olson, now his wife. Ladies and Gentlemen, Russell Polston has confessed to the deed and bitterly regrets it. But is he the real culprit? Is he not rather the victim of his social environment? His father is a notorious drunkard, who frequently abused his wife and his son. Little wonder that Russell was retarded. You have heard him speak. He stammers when he is nervous. He finds it hard to concentrate. He has never learnt how to discuss or solve a problem in an intelligent way. His father taught him the use of physical force. Russell's home was hell.

In 1981 he met Ginger at a party and fell for the pretty girl. Russell wanted to get married. Ginger didn't know what to do. Her parents were against the marriage. They felt their daughter could make a better match. This

uncertainty made his emotional instability worse. He suffered from fits of jealousy. Ginger, in turn, made fun of Russell's jealousy.
Such was the situation when the two went for a dance to the "Go and Get" bar in Newcastle on December 19. After two dances with the defendant, Ginger danced with Mr Hingston, a businessman from Shrewdburgh. Russell went to the bar counter and consumed five large whiskies, while helplessly observing Ginger flirt with Mr Hingston. The remainder of the story is known to you.
Ladies and Gentlemen,
I am sure you will pass a fair judgement on this man, who is a simple victim of his love and devotion. He was provoked by Ginger Polston, and she knows it. Would she otherwise have married him?
I am convinced that you will bear all this in mind when you walk through the door of the jury room and make your decision about the future life, the marriage and the happiness of Mr and Mrs Polston. Give their love a future.

3.5 – –

4. – –

7 BRAVE NEW WORLD

1. **Language**

1.1 "bemoan": "be-" makes transitive verbs out of nouns, adjectives, verbs. belittle – herabsetzen, heruntermachen, schmälern; bedevil – komplizieren, erschweren; bereave – berauben (archaic!); bespeak – verraten, erkennen lassen; besiege – belagern; besmirch – beschmutzen (fig., lit.); beset – bedrängen; befriend – sich annehmen (syn. help).

1.2 Chinese, Danish, French, Hungarian, Irish, Italian, Polish, Russian, Spanish, Swiss.

1.3 **Answers to "IT PAYS TO ENRICH YOUR WORD POWER**

1. **phase** – B: A stage of development or change; a particular aspect; as, the pioneering *phase* of the western states; a *phase* of the economy. Greek *phainesthai* (to appear).
2. **faze** – A: To upset, worry, disturb; as, Nothing seems to *faze* her. English dialectical *feeze* (to drive away).
3. **oral** – B: Spoken; by, of, or in the mouth; as, an *oral* report; *oral* thermometer. Latin *os* (mouth).

11. **cue** – C: Hint; guiding suggestion; an actor's signal; as, The music was the actor's *cue* to enter. In 16th- and 17th-century plays, a "Q (pronounced *kyoo*) was used to indicate a character's entrance.
12. **queue** – D: A line of people awaiting their turn; as, a *queue* at a movie theater. Latin *cauda* (tail).
13. **complacent** – A: When someone is very self-satisfied or

4. **aural** – A: Received through the ear or the sense of hearing. Latin *auris* (ear). The constant loud noise produced *aural* damage.
5. **censor** – B: Official empowered to examine all written and spoken material and to suppress whatever is considered unacceptable. Latin *censere* (to consider).
6. **censer** – C: A container for burning incense. Old French *censier.*
7. **elusive** – D: Tending to slip away; difficult to understand or perceive; as, an *elusive* thought; an *elusive* fragrance. Latin *eludere* (to deceive).
8. **illusive** – A: Not real; based on a false or misleading idea; deceptive; as, *illusive* dreams of instant wealth. Latin *illusio* (a mocking).
9. **acclamation** – D: Enthusiastic approval by loud applause, cheering, shouts. Latin *ad-* (to) and *clamare* (cry out). The stock market's record high was greeted with *acclamation.*
10. **acclimation** – D: An adaptation; becoming accustomed to a new climate or environment; as, the explorer's *acclimation* to the Arctic. Latin *ad-* (to) and *clima* (climate).

smug, he is said to be *complacent.* Latin *com* (an intensive) and *placere* (to please).

14. **complaisant** – B: When a person is *complaisant,* he wants to be obliging, to please, or to go along. Origin the same as *complacent.*
15. **discreet** – B: Tactful; prudent; using good judgment in delicate situations; as, a *discreet* reply. Latin *dis-* (apart) and *cernere* (to separate).
16. **discrete** – A: Separate; distinct; unrelated. Origin the same as *discreet.* They presented three *discrete* views of the same event.
17. **illicit** – D: Unlawful; not legal; as, *illicit* trading in stolen goods. Latin *illicitus* (not allowed).
18. **elicit** – A: To evoke; draw out, as, A joke may *elicit* a smile; The inquiry *elicited* important facts. Latin *e-* (out) and *lacere* (to entice).
19. **assent** – A: Consent or agreement; acceptance; as, the jurors' *assent.* Latin *ad-* (to) and *sentire* (to feel).
20. **ascent** – C: The act of rising or ascending; as, the *ascent* of a balloon. Also, an upward slope. Latin *ad-* (to) and *scandare* (to climb).

Vocabulary Ratings

20–18 correct . . . Master (exceptional)

17–12 correct . . . Player (excellent)

11–9 correct . . . Novice (good)

1.4 **Answers**

arrival – departure, bachelor – spinster, buyer – seller, doctor – patient, fear – courage, fullness – emptiness, hate – love, health – disease, hunger – satiety, lady – gentlemen, landing – takeoff, laugther – cry(ing), listener – narrator, order – obedience, pride – humility, producer – consumer, professional – amateur, sadness – joy, merriment, servant – master, takeoff – touchdown.

2.1

Our time	*Brave New World*
viviparous birth	decanting from test tubes
children raised by parents	children raised in State Conditioning Centres
education (parents and state)	conditioning and hypnodaedia (state)
family	abolition of family: "everybody belongs to everybody else"
emotions	no emotions
love and sex	only sex
sex for procreation, emotional bonding and fun	sex only for fun
different nations	world state
instability and development	stability and stasis

2.2 – –

2.3
1) "Stability. No civilization without social stability. No social stability without individual stability" (l. 68)
2) "Fortunate boys! . . . No pains have been spared to make your lives emotionally easy – to preserve you, so far as that is possible, from having emotions at all." (l. 91)
3) "These . . . are unpleasant facts; I know it. But, then, most historial facts *are* unpleasant." (l. 19)
4) "But everyone belongs to every one else", he concluded, citing the hypnopaedic proverb. (l. 48)

2.4 Family: natural right: own children. Changing these human rights would be very difficult. That's why most anti-utopian societies that install new institutions are preceded by great revolutionary wars. *Brave New World:* "Nine-Years War".

2.5 – –

2.6 Cf. annotations!

3.1 That depends on one's standpoint. To what extent can we take history as a means of proving – or denying – a case? To our (Western) eyes Communists rewrite history in order to justify their interpretation of it (cf. *1984!*), and vice versa! However, calling historical facts 'unpleasant' is surely no sign of objectivity; it is the kind of assessment that will lead to the falsification of history or the banishment of it from public memory – which is, instead, a sign of weakness.

3.2 Art. 6 Grundgesetz: family = basic unit of community and state, child-rearing: right of parents, choice of school: right of parents too, protection of individual against state.

3.3 It surely is an anti-utopia (cf. vol. 1, p. 56): "negative ideal", maybe not nightmarish, but superficial, no individuality, no family but all-powerful state, no history, no life in the full sense of the word: ups and downs, love and hate, loneliness and togetherness, strife and zest; complete standstill (stasis), no movement, literature banned as individualizing, man = machinomorphized.

4. Text 1:

What breaks up the young marriages? Lack of sex? Lack of communication? Lack of freedom? A lack of something in the institution of marriage itself? Nonsense. It is lack of money. Or, to put it another way, lack of preparation for the job of supporting a family.

Text 2:

In response to the question "What do you regard as the most satisfying thing about your family life?" the qualities mentioned most often were, in order of preference: children, closeness, being together, loving atmosphere, companionship, doing things together, communication, good marriage, religion, helping one another, getting along, being happy, caring, a healthy family and security. Three in every four women still think the ideal life-style is to be married and have kids.

Grammar

Fill in the right prepositions:

1. Another student officiously showed . . . his learning.
2. They had not yet learned to draw the distinction . . . smut and science.
3. He was overwhelmed . . . confusion
4. In those days children were always brought . . . by their parents.
5. Home was a rabbit-hole, reaking . . . emotion.
6. Mothers brooded . . . their children.
7. Every one belongs . . . every one else.
8. The machines must keep . . . turning
9. Thousands of people starved . . . death.
10. No pains have been spared to preserve you . . . having emotions.

Translate the following sentences:

1. The repetitions had made them accept the statement.
2. Don't keep his fordship waiting!

3. I had to wait four weeks before she would let me have her.
4. I'll get it done for you.
5. We'll have your photo taken
6. We had our car stolen.
7. She had the children leave the playground.
8. Laß das Feuer nicht ausgehen!
9. Laß mich los!
10. Ich muß mir die Haare schneiden lassen.
11. Laß mich in Ruhe!
12. Cäsar ließ eine Brücke bauen.
13. Jedes Geräusch ließ sie hochfahren.
14. Ich lasse mein Zimmer tapezieren.

Solution

1. 1 off, 2 between, 3 with (auch: by), 4 up, 5 with, 6 over, 7 to, 8 on, 9 to, 10 from.
2. machten sie akzeptieren, bewirkten, daß . . ., 2: laß ihn nicht warten, 3: ich mußte warten, bevor sie mich ließ, 4: ich werde es für sie machen lassen, veranlassen, daß . . ., 5: wir werden dich fotografieren lassen, 6: unser Auto wurde gestohlen, auch: wir ließen unser Auto stehlen, 7: sie vertrieb die Kinder, schickte sie weg, jagte sie weg, 8: don't let the fire go out, 9: Let me go, 10: I must have my hair cut, 11: leave me alone, 12: had a bridge built, caused/ordered a bridge to be built, 13: made her start, 14: I'm having my room decorated.

8 HUNGER IS . . .

Assignments

1. The subject: The hungry masses in the UDCs (= underdeveloped countries), in particular the hungry children.
   The problem is compared with the nuclear holocaust in Hiroshima in 1945 where approximately 100,000 people were killed. The reason for making this comparison is to give the reader a concrete idea of the size of the catastrophe.
2. a) 500 million people do not get enough food every day.
   b) 40,000 children die for hunger-related diseases every day.
   c) The production of corn (wheat, rye, maize) and rice is sufficient to provide every person on earth with 3,000 calories a day.
3. First of all, they're collecting money which they will spend
   a) on food and medication, their transport to the areas where they are needed and their distribution
   b) on financing and organizing educational programs, industrialization, cultivation of the soil, etc. (Cf. topic 9, *MW* 2, pp. 69 ff.)

4. Some reasons:
   a) the birthrate is still much higher than the deathrate
   b) industrialization is advancing too slowly because of a lack of trained and skilled workers
   c) cultivation of soil is too slow due to the shortage of fertilizer and machinery
   d) erosion of the soil because of 1) the climate (droughts), 2) destruction of vegetation (through grazing goats and camels: Sahel; cutting down trees: Asia and South America), 3) construction of dams and poor use of irrigation systems (loss of fertilizing mud: Assuan dam; wasting surface water: Lybia)
   e) destruction of harvests by floods and insects
5. a) In his essay Ditfurth states that the 40,000 children who die of hunger every day in the UDCs would make the situation worse if they survived and had children. This cynical truth results – according to Ditfurth – from the wrong policies of organizations like *Misereor, Brot für die Welt,* and others that restrict themselves to the collection of money and the purchase and distribution of food, and thus help alleviate the guilt of the citizens of rich countries. Instead, these organisations should fight for birth control which is – according to Ditfurth – the only foreseeable way to avoid an unprecedented catastrophe in the near future.
   One result of this "moral absolution" is the waste of immense sums on armament in the industrialized states.
   Finally, Ditfurth attacks the Roman Catholic church which – in his opinion – pursues a hypocritical policy: on the one hand it calls for donations to save hungry children from starvation, on the other hand it forbids its followers the use of contraceptives.
   b) – –
   c) (Note: this task does not mean that the authors of this book identify with Dithfurth's contradictory and rather sophistical arguments. We simply wanted to prevent students copying the arguments used in the letters on p. 67 of *MW* 2.)

   Dear Sirs,
   Congratulations to Hoimar von Ditfurth for his honest and courageous article printed in the last number of your magazine. It was high time that somebody proved how overpopulation and starvation cannot be solved by the sending of money to the UDCs. Financial aid has been granted these countries for at least 35 years now, and what has been achieved? From decade to decade the number of people dying from hunger has actually grown, and will continue to grow until the governments of the UDCs are prepared to convince their people that a family of only one or two children means a better life for them and for their children. Nobody should regard this as impossible. The Chinese have demonstrated that a reduction in the birthrate can be achieved and

starvation overcome without money from the West. Why are others unable to do the same?
Yours sincerely,

6. a) Hoimar von Ditfurth is in error when he thinks that the problem of hunger can be solved by birthcontrol – as it were by means of the "pill". The poor results of such programs in India have clearly proved this. The essential prerequisite for a reduction in population pressure is the creation of economic and social conditions which diminish parents' dependence upon their children in old age. Only enforced sterilization and a consequent brutalization of society would be an alternative. Ditfurth's attack on non-governmental organisations, which are gaining more and more importance in developing policies, is utterly exaggerated and quite untenable. On the whole, their work must be considered as very positive.

   Hoimar von Ditfurth's attempt to reveal the hypocrisy of the campaigns for the hungry is irritating because his very proper conclusions are based on arguments which are not only provocative and misanthropic but also false. He is wrong to claim that children starved in the Third World today imply a decline in population growth tomorrow. The more children die, the more children will be born.

   b) – –

9 OVERCOMING OVERPOPULATION AND STARVATION IN UNDER-DEVELOPED COUNTRIES

Introducing the Topic

Assignments:

1. The chart shows that population growth was very slow between 8000 BC and 1650 AD. This was due to the high death rate. From then on the population has grown at an ever-increasing speed because of better medical treatment and hygiene, which have prolonged life-expectancy considerably all over the world. Thus, the growth rate of world population has accelerated tremendously since 1650. While mankind took 8000 years to grow from 5 million to 200 million, and another 1650 years to grow to 500 million, it doubled its numbers in the period between 1650 and 1850. At the moment, it doubles roughly every 35 years: in 1945, there were 2.3 billion humans, in 1982, 4.6 billion.
2. If present growth rate continued we could expect:
   in the year 2000: ~ 6.6 billion
   2050: ~ 13.5 billion
   2500: 3,000 billion (three thousand!)
   3000: astronomical

3. These figures are not realistic. More realistic estimates say that the growth of world population could come to a stop in the year 2100 or 2150. On the basis of these estimates the number of the inhabitants on the planet earth would become stable at around 15–20 billion.

   The reasons for this development:

   Population growth in industrialized countries (cf. *MW,* vol. 2, p. 32: *Fewer Babies in Europe*) has shown that fertility declines with increasing industrialization because

   a) industrialized states provide sufficient social security for old age.
   b) the number of women with jobs increases considerably.
   c) large families, which make it impossible for a woman to have a job, lower living standards and hamper possible social advance.
   d) children jeopardize a leisurely life-style, i.e. a life without additional responsibilities; they restrict spare time, add to noise, etc.

   Experts therefore expect a similar development in the long run in UDCs, provided that industrialization, social security, and living standards can be raised.

4. *Conclusions to be drawn:*

   a) population growth cannot continue as at present because it would mean more starving people, more poverty, more slum-filled cities, more unemployment, etc.
   b) industrialized states must help UDCs develop into semi-industrialized or industrialized states, and thus help them overcome overpopulation and starvation.

WORKSHEET

1.1.1 de-; dis-; il-; im-; in-; ir-; non-; un-

1.1.2 inadequate; non-commissioned; to discontinue; incompetent; unemployment; inequality; to de-escalate; illegal; disloyal; immoral; to demobilize; irresistible; irreversible; dissatisfaction; unsocial

1.2.1 It means “the small quantity of food people currently have available”.

1.2.2 It means “a way of life characterized by hard work and striving for higher living standards”.

The expression reminds Americans of their forefathers' fight to push back the frontier, i.e. the borderline between uninhabited wilderness and civilization. Life on the frontier was pursued in the hopes of more and better land, more independence and freedom, more self-realization, and above all of higher living standards.

1.3 American *vocabulary:* frontier: BE hardly ever uses this word in this meaning (cf. 1.2).

American *spelling:* “a” for “ou”: labor; “l” for “ll”: modeled

American *grammar:* in order to help break (BE prefers: to help to break)

1.4.1./2	assistants:	helpers
	assistance:	help, support
	attendants:	servants, persons who accompany an important person
	attendance:	act of attending (waiting upon s.o.; serving s.o.; being present at)
	circumstance:	condition, fact, etc. connected with an event or person
	confidence:	trust
	currents:	streams of water
	currants:	small, sweet, dried, seedless grapes used in cakes, pudding, etc.
	experiments:	tests
	insurance:	safeguard against loss, provision against sickness, death, etc. in return for regular payments
	maintenance:	taking action to preserve (a machine) in good order
	presents:	gifts
	presence:	being present
	resistance:	act of withstanding action or effect of s.th.

1.5 – –

2.1.1 Otherwise unemployment, poverty, hunger, etc. will not be overcome.

2.1.2 If there is no social security for old people they will tend to have many children. This in turn, raises the mortality rate because these children cannot all be nourished. On the other hand, social security means fewer children and a lower mortality rate.

2.1.3 First, they need money to buy agricultural machinery to increase productivity. Fertilizers and pesticides must be bought to improve the soil and control pests. The land must be watered, so wells and irrigation systems need to be built. Lorries are necessary for the transport of crops to warehouses and roads will have to be construed.

2.1.4 To create stable economies in countries lacking raw materials, a minimum of industrialization is required to provide jobs for the masses. Only people with jobs can afford to buy agricultural products. Without customer's demand, however, the agricultural sector is doomed to ruin because there is no motivation for the farmer to invest, work hard and produce more than he needs for the upkeep of his own family.

2.1.5 They should be concentrated on the manufacture of articles that a) are easily made (furniture, clothing, etc.); b) can be manufactured from imported parts (refrigerators, bikes, sewing machines, etc.); c) are labour-intensive

2.1.6 Reasons: a) the raw materials needed are not available.
b) the environment would be completely contaminated.

Possible objections: a) nobody knows for sure how many resources are still undiscovered (large reserves are probably to be found at the South Pole, and in Canada and Sibiria); b) new soft industries (based on high-tech) are going to become important, if not dominant; c) extraction of raw materials on other planets

2.1.7 They are to achieve the standard of a so-called "semideveloped" country. Reaching the standard of the ODCs would be too costly and would trigger off the disadvantages mentioned in 2.1.6. The ODCs, on the other hand, should not raise their living standards, but should even lower them slightly; people in the ODCs should change their life-styles, i.e. they should be content with what they have, instead of striving for more and more.

2.2.1 Part 1: ll. 1–7: Population Control Checks Poverty in UDCs
Part 2: ll. 8–15: The Importance of More Social Security
Part 3: ll. 16–28: Measures to Improve Agriculture
Part 4: ll. 29–38: The Importance of Industrialization in UDCs and Some Suggestions for its Realization.
Part 5: ll. 19–55: Future Economic Standards in Today's UDCs and ODCs.

2.2.2 neutral; clear; sober; nominal.
Justification: the speech level is neither formal nor colloquial (see also MW 2, pp. 126/127).
The contents of the text are easily comprehensible because the style is clear and sober. There are no obscure expressions which might be difficult to understand; the sentence structure is predominantly *simple* (few dependent clauses); emotional words are rarely used. Since there are few dependent clauses the text's style is predominantly nominal, i.e. the authors use a large number of nouns, pronouns, and gerunds.

2.2.3 The text is predominantly expository, i.e. it presents a problem and *explains* ways in which it can be overcome.
a) false; b) false; c) true; d) true; e) false; f) true; g) false

3.1 The authors' plans for improvements in agriculture and the creation of some basic industries in UDCs are certainly not utopian. Their analysis of the situation is undoubtedly correct; the practical measures they suggest to solve the problems are not too far-fetched; they understand that – for several reasons – it is impossible and undesirable for UDCs to reach a living standard equal to that of ODCs. However, it is obviously unrealistic to imagine that the problems of the UDCs could be solved at the expense of the ODCs. First of all, democratic governments in the ODCs can hardly force their citizens to change their life-styles or even lower their living-standards. Moreover, a lower level of industrialization in the ODCs is not necessarily the right recipe for an increase in financial support for the UDCs, or for the improvement of the latter's sales in world markets: the prices of their products are, anyway, unrivalled.

3.2 Some arguments:

Yes: a) their population growth makes any financial support futile.
b) financial support diminishes their need to help themselves.
c) countries should solve their own problems.

No: a) money has helped and helps every day to save thousands of lives.
b) the former colonial powers have a moral obligation to the UDCs, because they exploited them in the past.
c) it's our task as Christians to give all possible help.
d) UDCs may be prospective business partners. Raising their living-standards could mean opening up future new markets.

3.3 Overpopulation and starvation can certainly lead to dictatorships; indeed, they have already produced dictatorships in most UDCs. However, it is unlikely that overpopulation and starvation in Asia and Africa will lead to a world-wide dictatorship as it is represented in *Brave New World.* It is more likely to cause a world-wide war between the ODCs and the UDCs.

3.4 Suggestion: If students want to learn more about this idea, which recommends a drastic reduction in the consumption of meat in ODCs because it takes 16 pounds of grain and soya beans to produce just 1 pound of beef in the United States today, have a student prepare a paper on the book *Diet for a Small Planet,* Ballantine paperback, New York 1982, by Frances Moore-Lappé. It is perhaps interesting that Moore-Lappé is a graduate of Earlham College, Richmond/Indiana (class of 1966), a small Midwestern *Quaker* College. Some professors teaching at this college were and are firm vegetarians. Among them was Dr Hans Buchinger, who taught Latin and Greek there in the 1950's and 1960's. He, incidentally, was one of the Buchingers who run a special clinic for dietetics on Lake Constance.

3.5 Reasons: The overproduction of food (meat, grain, fruit, milk products) in the ODCs would lead to fall in prices on the world-market and on domestic markets unless such prices were artificially maintained. To keep prices up, food is sometimes deliberately destroyed by farmers or governments. More often it is bought by governments and stored in warehouses and cold-storage depots. If that weren't done many farmers would go out of business. However, storing food costs taxpayers gigantic amounts of money every year. Why then is the food not shipped to the UDCs? Shipping the surplus food to the UDCs would lead to even higher outlays for tonnage. Moreover, most UDCs do not have enough storage capacity, or the necessary infrastructure, to distribute the food fast enough before it goes bad. Therefore it happens now and then that governments in the UDCs sell such foodstuffs to other countries, like the Soviet Union, at prices far below world market prices. What can be done? Not much. It is, of course, possible to pay premiums to farmers to encourage voluntary cut in their production, but such a policy won't help the hungry of the world. The only advantage of such a policy would seem to be that fields lying fallow could be afforested, which would contribute to the improvement of our environment. (Cf. also *MW* 3 for more reading matter on this topic.)

4.1.1 It shows the globe totally overcrowded with humans.

4.1.2/3 He obviously compares the earth with an overpopulated bee-hive. As bees leave their hive when it is overcrowded, so the humans will soon be so densely packed that they will apparently be forced to do what the bees do. Of course, that's a gross exaggeration (see p. 54). In particular, we are able to use our brains to solve the problem. But – as we have already learnt – it requires a desperate effort to overcome indifference, egoism, prejudice, stupidity, inefficiency, and corruption, all of which hinder the achievement of zero population growth.

4.1.4.1/2 The baby, of course, serves to illustrate and underline the message of the cartoon: it has no place to land, or to grow. The fact that the baby is floating *above* and not *below* the globe is possibly an ironic reference to the wide-spread conviction that children are "a blessing from heaven".

10 THE WANTING SEED

1.1 sorrow: grief; glittering: shining; small: tiny; habit: custom; amiable: benevolent; quick: fast, rapid; evident: apparent; drenched: soaked; severe: strict; share: ration; pretty: handsome; menace of fertility: threat of fecundity; tremble: shudder; stare: gaze; dislike: distaste.

1.2 a) Employees of the Ministry of Agriculture made an official call that caused Beatrice-Joanna a lot of disappointment and sadness.
b) He was so used to the job that it was easy for him.
c) That sort of infection spreads at tremendous speed.
d) A final slap to show that he considered the matter ended.
e) A young man entered the lift.
f) Don't forget to take into consideration the consequences for the whole nation.

2.1 a) Mrs Foxe goes to see a doctor because . . . her little son is dead and she needs the death certificate.

b) Dr Acheson tries to soothe her by . . . telling her that she will get a condolence in cash and that she will get her son back (in another form, though).

c) Compared with a doctor's task in our time Dr Achesons is different in as much as . . . he cares rather for the population as a whole than for the individual, he doesn't regret losing "a mouth to feed" but works to ease the population strain.

d) Mrs Foxe is nearly sick when she sees the embracing pair . . . because she disapproves of a world that "diverts sex from its natural end".

e) Human life is of little value in that future world. This is shown
1st, by the men of the Ministry of Agriculture because . . . they sing and whistle as they "reclaim phosphorus",
2nd, by the doctor because . . . he is happy that there is "one mouth less to feed",
3rd, by the "condolence" because . . . it consists of cash.

f) The Great Britain of that future world is a racially mixed country because . . . much of the overpopulation in other parts of the world spills into Europe and Great Britain.

g) Mrs Foxe is atavistic in so far as . . . she is by mental and physical shape still womanly and feminine in the 20th century sense, she emanates an air of fecundity.

h) "Dognose" is a pun on "God knows" and this expression shows that Christian religion has been discredited because . . . fertility, human life and children rank high in Christian faith.

2.2 a) Dr Acheson: fat gelding of an Anglo-Saxon, benevolent and cheerful, womanly and gentle.

Miss Herschorn: Teutonico-Chinese, a plain thin girl with dog's eyes and very lank straight black hair, quick movements, quacking voice.

Mrs Foxe: old-fashioned (not modern), handsome woman of 29, opulence of haunches, healthy and fecund, womanly, atavistic.

INVERSION: Dr Acheson = womanly type, Miss Herschorn = teutonic, unwomanly.

b) Future society: tiny doctor's office high buildings: little space because of overpopulation; motherhood: lower orders: class society, only one child allowed; hair fashion: straight and fringed, perfume and lipsticks for men only; homosexuality encouraged; corpses for agriculture; advanced technology: audiograph; racial mixture; degeneration: artificial teeth.

3.1 Contents parallel that of story: human beings serve as food to other human beings, in the song directly, in the story indirectly.

3.2 "Admonitory" because they want to utter a warning; in this case a warning against overpopulation. "Satire" because the story evokes feelings of contempt, scorn, dislike towards the conditions depicted.
An indirect effect, of course, is that we feel reassured that, after all, our world is not (yet) so bad.

3.3 Our extract: social problems of living in crowded conditions. Exhaustion of resources: *Planet of Fear*, vol. 1, p. 120; *The Space Merchants*, vol. 1, p. 116; *Paradise*, additional text Lehrerbegleitband, vol. 1, p. 90.
Destruction of environment: *Where Do the Children Play*, vol. 1, p. 58; *Space Merchants*, loc. cit.

3.4 Possible points to ponder: apparent inefficiency of existing means of contraception, at least in LDCs; industrialized countries pay child allowances increasing with the number of children; prevailing pre-industrial notions and conditions stronger: sex is easiest and often only pleasure; lack of education, children = insurance for old age and illness; only China tries to handle the problem by allocating the allowance in inverse proportion: the more children the smaller the allowance.

3.5 Two world wars, countless minor wars always being waged somewhere on the globe, rising economic, ecological and social problems, increasing danger of disaster, hardly leave any room for hopeful, idealistic and optimistic speculations: man seems incapable of coping with his problems.

4.1 Article: decline of population in Europe; *Wanting Seed:* increase of population in Great Britain. This, however, need not be a contradiction as the text of the novel shows that there has been an enormous influx of non-Europeans into Europe and Great Britain, and a tremendous mixing of the different races.

4.2 Population growth in Europe around 1750. It ran parallel to the Industrial Revolution, which started in Great Britain. There is an interaction between population growth and Industrial Revolution: The Industrial Revolution is at the same time precondition and consequence of the population growth. The population growth was (and in LDCs still is) due to the dropping of the mortality rate. According to historians, the following factors account for this phenomenon in Great Britain:

- favourable conditions of domestic and foreign politics (stable social order, no or few wars);
- higher level of education (greater control of production and supply of food, clothes, housing);
- sanitary factors (water supply, sewage system);
- medical factors (better prevention and treatment of disease);
- improvement of economic conditions (increase of wages, substitution of the economy of subsistence by the free market of a capitalist economy; investments in communication systems);

– social reforms (improvement of working conditions, fixing of minimum wages, social services and national health service).

4.3 Gaps: "... similar roots: high living costs; ... towards marriage, sex and children; increased contraception; ... calls "the economic and social anxiety that haunts us all."

Grammar

1. Translate the following sentences:
   a) Beatrice-Joanna sobbed, but the man went on singing, having no feeling of his business, *custom having made it in him a property of easiness.*
   b) He stood there, his heart beating.
   c) She looked at him, her knees trembling.
   d) The war being ended, they went home.
   e) Weather permitting, we'll have a picnic.
   f) The teacher having finished, the class calmed down.

   What strikes you about these participal constructions? Which speech level do they belong to? (cf. ch 14) Translate them into colloquial English!
2. Translate:
   "I know, I know. I blame myself"
   The English language has only a few verbs which must always take the reflexive pronoun. Work them out:
   a) Die Kinder waschen sich gerade.
   b) Zieh den Mantel an, um dich warm zu halten!
   c) Herr Brown stellte sich vor.
   d) Er beschäftigte sich mit allen möglichen Arbeiten.
   e) Er ist stolz auf seine naturwissenschaftlichen Kenntnisse.
   f) Wenn du dich nicht benehmen kannst, mußt du gehen!
   g) Ich habe leider verschlafen.
   h) Er hat sich irgendwo im Haus versteckt.
   i) Die Bücher verkaufen sich gut.
   k) Die ganze Familie versammelte sich.
   l) Fühl dich wie zu Hause!

Solution

1. a) Beatrice-Joanna schluchzte, aber der Mann fuhr fort zu singen, er fühlte nichts bei seiner Arbeit, er hatte sich so an sie gewöhnt, daß sie ihm leicht von der Hand ging. (Quotation from *Shakespeare's Hamlet,* V, 1, 69)
   b) Er stand da mit pochendem Herzen.
   c) Sie schaute ihn mit zitternden Knien an.
   d) Nach dem Ende des Krieges gingen sie nach Hause.
   e) Wenn das Wetter es erlaubt, machen wir ein Picknick.

f) Nachdem der Lehrer fertig war (geendet hatte), beruhigte sich die Klasse. Absolute participles (unverbundene Partizipien), literary style; colloquial English:

a) he had got used to it
b) . . . with his heart beating
c) . . . with trembling knees.
d) After the war . . .
e) If the weather is fine . . .
f) After the teacher (had) finished . . .

2. "Ich weiß, ich weiß. Ich mach mir deswegen ja auch Vorwürfe."
a) The children are washing.
b) Put on your coat to keep yourself warm!
c) Mr Brown introduced himself.
d) He busied himself with all kinds of sundries/jobs.
e) He prides himself on his scientific knowledge.
f) If you can't behave, you must go!
g) I'm afraid I overslept (myself).
h) He has hidden somewhere in the house.
i) The books are selling well.
k) The whole family gathered.
l) Make yourself at home!

11 CASTAWAY

WORKSHEET

1.1 a) to be crucial *for/to; on* each occasion; I lay burning *with;* to spend money *on;* to dictate s.th. *to* s.b.; to emerge *from* s.th.; to contribute *to; in* different ways; a book *on* plants; to have no great knowledge *of* s.th.; to have no great knowledge *of* doing s.th.; to be envious *of* s.th./s.b.; if we look *at* our time . . . *with* the eyes of; to be intent *on* survival; our efforts *at* s.th.; to be tied *to;* the sea is poison *for/to* sores; to be fit *for*; to fit *into* the environment; to gain: to gain (experience), to gain *in* (weight), to gain *on* (the other cars in a race), to gain s.th. *from* (a stay in a foreign country), to gain s.b. *for* (a work, position); *for* this purpose; *to* the book *with* interest; it is far *from* being rubbish.

1.2 a) no; b) yes; c) no; d) no; e) no; f) no; g) yes; h) yes

1.3.1

to put into one's head	to get a fixed idea
to put s.b. out	(here) to upset
to put at ease	to put in a good mood to make s.o. relaxed

to put on weight	to gain weight
to put s.o. into the embarrassing position	to bring s.o. into the . . .
to put one's foot down	to take up a strong position
to be put out of countenance	to lose one's composure
to put into s.o's mind	to remind s.o. of
to put an end to s.th.	to bring s.th. to an end
to put s.o.'s back up	to annoy s.o. (by saying or doing s.th. bad or offensive)
to put a good face on	to give the appearance of being satisfied with s.th.
to put on one's thinking cap	to think about, and try to solve, a problem
to put the matter to s.o.	to confront s.o. with the problem
to put s.o. up	to accommodate s.o.
to put s.th. to other use	to make use of s.th. in another way
to put one's case down	to set one's case (= bag) on the floor
to put it differently	to say it in other words
to put up for sale	to offer for sale
to put s.o. into difficulties	to give s.o. trouble
putting it mildly	to say the least (of it)
I have put my time at your disposal	I have given you my time
to be put into this world	to be brought into this world
to put s.o.'s wind up	to cause s.o. to become nervous, to feel fear or worry
to be put off	to be discouraged
to put two and two together	to realize or work out something from what one sees, hears etc.
to put the lid on s.th.	to be the final blow to s.th. (very unsatisfactory)
to put up with s.o.	to deal with s.o. patiently, to have patience with s.o.
to put s.th. across to s.o.	to inform s.o. of s.th., to communicate with s.o. successfully
to put queer notions into one's head	to start thinking of strange ideas
to put o.s. in s.o.'s place	to imagine what it would be like to be s.o.
to put s.th. right with s.o.	to inform s.o. about the fact that one has made a mistake
to put s.o. into a happy frame of mind	to make s.o. feel happy
to put s.th. through	to bring s.th. to a successful end

1.3.4 a) up; b) up; c) out; d) on; e) on; f) across/over; g) off; h) through; i) up with; j) down

1.4

	1	2	3	4	5	6	7	8	9	10	11	12	13	14	15	16	17	
1		1 P	2 U	3 S			4 H	A	G	G	5 A	6 R	7 D		8 A	I	9 D	1
2			10 S	U	11 N		E				12 T	U	I	N			O	2
3	13 M	E		14 R	E	T	R	E	15 A	16 T		S			17 T		T	3
4	O			18 R	A		O		19 C	A	20 S	T	21 A	22 W	A	23 Y		4
5	L		24 M	O	T	25 H	E	26 R		27 P	A		28 P	O	L	E	S	5
6	29 D	R	A	G		30 U	S	E	31 D		32 C	R	E	E	K	S		6
7			33 R	A	34 I	N		35 L	O	C	K						36 T	7
8	37 B	38 S		39 T	U	G		40 O	N			41 O	42 P	43 P	O	44 S	E	8
9	45 R	A	46 P	E		47 E	48 R	A		49 B	50 I	N	G	O		51 I	N	9
10	52 A	P	O		53 G	R	A	D	U	A	T	E		54 P	A	N	T	10
	1	2	3	4	5	6	7	8	9	10	11	12	13	14	15	16	17	

The title of the book is: *Robinson Crusoe*

2.1 Sense unit 1 (ll. 1–6): The Dictates of Nature
Sense unit 2 (ll. 7–12): The Stranger in the Mirror
Sense unit 3 (ll. 13–23): Longing for Rain
Sense unit 4 (ll. 25–40): Nature's Effect on the "Castaways'" Psyche
Sense unit 5 (ll. 41–72): Crime and Self-punishment

2.2 Their lives revolve around the conditions imposed by their environment.

2.3 Her face has probably changed because of the hardships the new environment imposes on her. In line 71 she refers to "a group of people on severe rations", i.e. she and G. were on emergency rations as well. That is why she calls the incident "an unforgivable sin" (l. 41). The text also shows that they are desperately hoping for rain.

2.4 Lack of food and water, the heat, mosquitoes and sandflies result in psychic and physical stress which, in turn, develops into open aggressiveness. The tensions are also intensified by Lucy's refusal to sleep with her "husband" (cf. Note on the Text). It doesn't become clear, however, whether this refusal has its origin in the stress they are exposed to or simply in the fact that Lucy doesn't like her partner well enough. The text allows both interpretations (cf. ll. 30–33).

2.5 It shows that exposure to psychic and physical stress not only leads to aggressiveness but can also cause people to forget civilized behaviour; . . . that people in extreme situations (e.g. suffering from hunger and thirst or extreme stress) can develop a radical egotism.

2.6 – –

2.7

Diary	Other part of the extract
Language more matter-of-fact; relatively few images (cocoons of thought, Parthian shot, gems);	Language more poetic; more images (banalities of routine; to wield an implacable baton; green soldiers; grey phantoms)
Alliteration: hardly any;	alliteration: to **f**lounder or **f**lourish; **f**ew inches . . . **f**ace . . . revealed **f**our or **f**ive times
Contrasts: hardly any;	Contrasts: flounder or flourish; night and day; time to labour and time to rest;
descriptive adjectives: relatively few	many descriptive adjectives

2.8 There is a number of similarities: a) the protagonists of both books live on an island far away from civilization; b) both books show that life without technology is not an idyll; c) that psychic and physical stress results in aggressiveness and hostility; d) both books represent man as the "tamed ape" who is always in danger of losing his veneer of civilization.

2.9 The story is "fascinating" because it shows the behaviour of two persons in unusual circumstances and unusual surroundings. It depicts ". . . such dreams as stuff is made of" (Note the interesting switch of the actual Shakespearian saying!), which means that Lucy Irvine's book offers the dreams out of which the ordinary "stuff" of reality is made.

"A self-searching tale . . . she is a born writer . . .", because the author underwent this experience to find out how she reacts to such a radically different environment and because – without ever having written a novel – she is able to describe this experience in a vivid manner.

On the other hand, the extract reveals the prose of a mediocre writer, drowning in her own clichés ("wielded an implacable baton", "green soldiers", "grey phantoms", etc.).

3.1.1 – –

3.1.2 *Translation:*

Schiffsbrüchig

Nach und nach, innerhalb und außerhalb der Banalitäten der Routinearbeiten, übernahm der Rhythmus von Tuin selbst die Führung. Sonne, Mond und Gezeiten führten ein unerbittliches Regiment, dirigierten jede unserer Bewegungen und schrieben uns vor, wann Zeit zu fischen, zu arbeiten und zu ruhen war. Und doch waren wir innerhalb dieser metronomischen

Einschränkungen frei zu schuften oder zu faulenzen und das Leben zu genießen. Um zu überlegen, muß man sich anpassen. Zeichnet sich erst einmal das Muster der Anpassung ab, dann kann man erkunden, wo die Freiheiten liegen . . .
Ich glaube, im Verlauf der ersten elf Monate auf Tuin habe ich die paar Zentimeter meines Gesichtes, die der Spiegel zeigte, gerade vier- oder fünfmal gesehen. Doch bei jeder dieser Gelegenheit legte ich ihn schnell beiseite. Die Person, die ich im Spiegel entdeckte, war eine Fremde, jemand, den anzuschauen mir schwerer fiel als in ihm zu leben. Die Tatsache, daß sich wegen der Spiegelgröße immer nur ein neugieriges Auge oder ein Teil einer braunen Wange oder der Nase genauer untersuchen ließ, verzerrte die Sache vielleicht noch zusätzlich.
Die sich verschlimmernde Wassersituation gab uns reichlich Anlaß zur Besorgnis. Eine Zeitlang, ungefähr sechs Wochen, segelten täglich große, graue Wolken über die Insel. Das aufschießende Gemüse im Garten war in einem Stadium, in dem regelmäßige Wässerung lebensnotwendig war. Von meinem Platz am Feuer aus sah ich G. jeden Morgen aus dem Zelt auftauchen und sofort zum Himmel hochschaun.
„Eine große dort drüben“, rief er und deutete über Tuins Hügel hinweg. „Könnt heut einen Schauer geben.“
Jetzt, wo er nicht länger in der Lage war, die grünen Soldaten zu gießen, schaute er den ganzen Tag hindurch zum Himmel hoch und hoffte. Beide stimmten wir darin überein, daß überhaupt keine Wolken besser wären als die quälende Lockung dieser nicht zu fassenden grauen Phantome, die über uns durch den Himmel huschten.

12 LORD OF THE FLIES

WORKSHEET

1 **Language**

1.1 Disentangle the following rows of letter-mixes and find two sentences with information about *Lord of the Flies.* The German words tell you which words of the annotations to find; the remaining letters give you the solution. The first sentence consists of six words, the second sentence of 15.

Example: (Kern) **C**L**O**O**R**RD**E:** look for the English word **core,** the remaining word is “Lord”.

Sentence no. 1: it instantly became a modern classic.

(jammern, heulen) W**I**H**IT**NE whine, it

(unerträglich) U**IN**NEN**S**DU**T**R**A**A**N**BL**TL**E**Y** unendurable, IN-STANTLY (gähnen) **B**Y**E**A**C**W**A**N**ME A** (two words left in here!) Yawn, BECAME A (mampfen, zermalmen, zerbeißen) **M**C**O**R**D**U**E**N**R**C**H**N crunch, MODERN

(abscheulich, gräßlich) A**C**B**L**O**A**M**S**I**S**NAIBL**C**E abominable, CLASSIC

Sentence no. 2: it was one of the most acute studies of child psychology in modern English fiction. (lärmend, lautstark) **I**C**T**LA**W**M**A**O**S**-RO**U**O**S**N**E** (3 words left) clamorous, IT WAS ONE

(zurückzucken) **O**F**F**T**L**H**E**I**N**M**C**O**H**S**T** (3 words left) flinch, OF THE MOST

(verrückt, wahnsinnig) **A**C**D**U**T**E**E**M**S**T**E**U**N**D**T**I**E**E**S**D**O**F (3 words left) demented, ACUTE STUDIES OF

(erschüttern, zertrümmern) **C**H**I**S**L**H**D**A**P**S**T**Y**T**C**H**E**O**L**R**O**G**Y (two words left) shatter, CHILD PSYCHOLOGY

(klopfen, pulsieren, pochen) TH**I**RO**N**B throb, IN

(Kralle, Klaue) **M**C**O**L**D**A**E**W**R**N claw, MODERN

(Fransen, Rand, Saum) **E**F**N**R**G**I**L**N**I**G**S**E**H** fringe, ENGLISH

(Marmor) **F**I**M**A**C**T**R**B**I**L**E**O**N**. marble, FICTION

1.2 Williams Golding has created a successful adventure story about a group of boys abandoned on a tropical island somewhere in the Pacific Ocean. They are the victims of a war which is still raging elsewhere. Golding shows how the boys adapt to the island, learning how to make fire, to build shelters, to hunt and to maintain discipline. Initially they relish their new freedom but under the strain of their total isolation they develop tensions which finally break out into conflict. They reject their first leader, replacing him by a boy who is better able to cope with the physical hardships of the island. The community they develop around him is aggressive but also prepared to accept his absolute authority. When rescue finally comes the boys have lost all touch with the 'civilised' values of their former existence. They have become like 'savages'.

1.3 Explanatory Answers

(the tasks and the answers have been taken from: *Preparation for the College-Level Examination Program,* Henry Regnery Company, Chicago 1972, p. 1 ff.)

SECTION 1: Correct and Effective Expression

1. (D) The sequence of tenses requires the past tense of the verb. Write *began.*
2. (B) An adverb is used to modify an adjective. Write *really modern.*
3. (E) No error.
4. (C) Never use *a* or *an* after *sort of, kind of, manner of, style of, or type of.* Say *what kind of dinner.*
5. In a past statement contrary to fact, the verb of the "if" clause is in the past perfect (had waited).

SECTION 2

1. (V). *Final outcome* is redundant.
2. (O) No error.
3. (G) The subject pronoun *it* has an indefinite antecedent. The word *cage,* though close to *it* is not logically the antecedent because the cage did not kiss the zoo attendant. Reword the sentence so that there is no question about what the antecedent is: *entered the cage of the monkey, it kissed him.*
4. (L) The expression *bolt from the blue* is trite.
5. (D) The word *formally* (meaning in a formal manner) should replace *formerly* (meaning previously).
6. (G) There is a dangling participle here. *Exhausted* is a participle that does not clearly modify anything in the sentence. Say *Since he was exhausted, the newspaper . . .*

2.1 – –

2.2 a) true, b) true, c) false: he ordered them to dance, d) false: they just shook and waved them, e) false: Roger did, f) true, g) false: it was Simon, h) false: about the parachutist, i) true, k) false: he was beaten to death.

2.3 Antagonism and even war on the island – (nuclear) war in the outside world.

2.4 Beast: human (esp. a child's) fear of and anguish at the unknown; fear, irrationality, power, evil; means of intimidation for Jack.

Lord: sacrifice to beast; baseness: pig and flies, dirt, uncivilized; religious need of man: ritual; appeasement of own conscience; Lord of the Flies: Beelzebub.

Parachutist: instrusion from and connection with outside/adult world: war and destruction and death.

Island: paradise destroyed by humans; natural surrounding for humans: adaptation (cf. outside world: reduction to natural, precivilized state).

These are, of course, just a few hints to work on. *Lord of the Flies* can be and has been interpreted from various points of view: psychological, sociological, ethological etc. (cf. 3.2)

3.1 Adventure story: tradition: ship-wrecked on an island, cf. *Robinson Crusoe, Gulliver's Travels, Coral Island.*

Fable: definition: ". . . a story, exemplifying a moral thesis, in which animals talk and act like human beings." There are no talking animals in *Lord of the Flies,* but a moral: civilization is but a thin layer easily broken, man is fundamentally a savage creature, sensibility and brains are not always the best means of survival.

Allegory: definition: ". . . undertakes to make a doctrine or thesis interesting or persuasive by converting it into a narrative in which the agents, and sometimes the setting as well, represent general concepts, moral qualities, or other abstractions." For the doctrine or thesis, see "fable"; the vehicle

of persuasion is the adventure plot. Thus, *Lord of the Flies* is a fine blend of all three elements: adventure story, fable, allegory.
(The definitions have been taken from: M H Abrams, *A Glossary of Literary Terms,* Holt, Rinehart and Winston, New York, London, 1964).

3.2 Politics: War, evacuation of a class of English school boys; elaboration of Hobbes' theory (in *Leviathan*) that man is a wolf to man ("homo homini lupus"), i.e. intrinsically selfish. Golding might be said to add that man is not capable of building lasting communities or of cultural achievement.
Anthropology: Is the evil or the good side in man stronger? What part does evil play in human life, individual or collective? Is Jack bad or just natural? Is he more likely than Ralph to ensure survival on the island?
Is there a question of "brawns vs. brains"? *Lord of the Flies* can be read as an elaboration on the conditio humana.
Morality: see above: 3.1.
Theology: Is there a need to adore a super-human entity? a god, a supernatural power? Is this so because there is such an entity? or because man feels a need to justify his doings by appealing to such entities?
Sociology/philosophy: study in group behaviour, esp. the behaviour of children: emulation of adults?, importance of bodily strength for the building of a juvenile community: war games (hunting of Ralph), courage tests (hunting of pig). Philosophy of survival: survival of the fittest: Jack's leadership.

3.3 Sf: frame: near future, World War III; interest: mankind (humankind) as such, not individual fates (boys on the island are types! Piggy: inventor, intellectual); moral message: depravity of man. *Lord of the Flies* could be called 'anthropological sf' (like Golding's novel *The Inheritors*).
Lord of the Flies might also be seen and interpreted as an anti-utopia (cf. vol 1, p. 56) in nuce: the incapacity for building lasting, good societies is inborn in human beings. An apt German counterpart to this thesis is N. Loacker's novel *Aipotu.*

4.1 *Coral Island:* pure adventure story
Robinson Crusoe: evolution from savagery to civilization
Lord of the Flies: 'devolution' from civilization to savagery.

4.2 Because *Lord of the Flies* is open to a variety of interpretations all kinds of definitions of aggression can be applied to it. The most appropriate definition, however is that of A. Mitscherlich: aggression is part of human nature, as human nature as such is dealt with in Golding's novel. Freud's theory holds true, too, of course; whereas the definition of aggression as reaction to frustration is probably the most inappropriate, although one might point out that the boys are perhaps frustrated because of their loss of civilization.

13 DREAMING THAT DREAM

1.1 **Superordinates:** *race and racism:* apartheid, blacks, colour, to desegregate, desegregation, ghetto life, negroes, race relationships, race relations, racial division, race war, racist, segregation, segregated, slaves, slave owners, supremacist, whites.

economic life: board rooms, corporate, corporations, to earn, economically mired, economic regime, economic share, economic standing, jobs, job deal, job market, management, managerial, managers, Reaganomics, recession, unemployment, to work.

1.2 1) labourer 2) to illustrate 3) oppression 4) negro 5) economic 6) liberalism 7) hypocrisy 8) apartheid 9) managerial 10) police 11) traditionally 12) oratory 13) nobility

Solution: Lionel Hampton (b. April 12, 1913, Louisville, Ky.), orchestra leader, brilliant musical improviser on the vibraphone, and an almost overwhelmingly extroverted performer; his irrepressible enthusiasm for his idiom regularly generated immense emotional responses from his audiences.

He was reared in Chicago and in 1928 became a professional musician, soon joining the band of Les Hite, then led by Louis Armstrong. While working as a drummer, Hampton experimented with the electrically amplified vibraphone (vibraharp) and recorded it for the first time in October 1930, with Louis Armstrong; the composition was "Memories of You." He became famous as a member of Benny Goodman's quartet from 1936 to 1940, after which he formed his own touring orchestra. In 1942 Hampton recorded the famous, rabble-rousing "Flyin' Home." He toured the world, and although his onstage manner at times threatened to overwhelm musical considerations, he always retained superb technical command and vigorous enthusiasm.

From: Encyclopaedia Britannica, Micropaedia IV, p. 879

1.3.1 Reagan + economics

1.3.2 alcoholiday: alcohol + holiday = a holiday on which much alcohol is consumed

brunch: breakfast + lunch = late morning meal instead of breakfast and lunch

cinemaddict: cinema + addict = person who likes to go to the cinema very often

dictaphone: dictation + telephone = machine that records and reproduces dictation

to electrocute: electro + execute = to execute in the electric chair

glob: globe + blob = a rounded mass of usu. large size (a ~ of rice)

guesstimate: guess + estimate = an approximate conjecture
happenstance: to happen + circumstance = a random event, incident
infanticipation: infant + anticipation = expectation of a baby
motel: motor + hotel = bungalow-type hotels situated on the highways
rotel: rolling + hotel = bus plus trailer which serves as accommodation for the night
rollathon: to roll + marathon: roller skate competition over a long distance
smog: smoke and fog = layer of smoke and fog over city
stagflation: stagnation + inflation = state of economy characterized by stagnation and inflation (normally it's either stagnation or inflation)
travelogue: travel + dialogue = a talk, lecture, article, or film on travel
wargasm: war + orgasm = a sudden outbreak of war
workaholic: work + alcoholic = person who is addicted to work, who can't live without work, as an alcoholic cannot live without alcohol

1.3.3 Some other blends:
brunnel: bridge + tunnel = type of possible future traffic connection between England and the Continent, combining a bridge with a tunnel
Chunnel: Channel + tunnel = another type of traffic connection between England and the Continent: a tunnel under the Channel
to chortle: to chuckle + to snort = to utter a low, deep laugh
fanimal: fan + animal = British football fan who behaves like an animal, football hooligan
worldgram: world + telegram = news of the world in telegram style
telex: teleprinter + exchange = international telegraph service using teleprinters exchanging material

1.4 a) over b) above c) over – over d) across e) above f) beyond – beyond g) over h) over i) beyond j) across

2.1 *Social situation of USA blacks in the 1950's and 1960's:* racial discrimination in almost all fields of life, such as: segregated public facilities (transport, toilets, swimming pools, schools, parks, etc.)
segregated private facilities (restaurants, job market, churches, housing)
politics (gerrymandering, disfranchisement, lack of representation in political bodies such as state assemblies, administration, police)
Social situation of the blacks today:

a) racial discrimination in few but important fields:
some schools in the South are still segregated, some churches are still segregated
inequalities in the job market (blacks tend to be the first to be dismissed; hardly any blacks in the board rooms)
gerrymandering still practised in some areas in the South

b) economic setbacks:

high unemployment rate
more blacks below the poverty line than at the end of the 1960's.

c) other social difficulties:
high illiteracy
ghetto life
corrosion of black family life (large number of births outside wedlock)

2.2 Negro movement of the Sixties:
Martin Luther King – – March on Washington, August 26, 1963 – – fight for freedom = equality – – white support of but also hostility to negro demands – –King's non-violent approach not always successful; nevertheless: success in important fields like civil rights and voting rights acts, greater black participation in politics, improvement of race relations in the South.

2.3 Mainly two aims: 1) abolishing abuses of disfranchisement like gerrymandering where it is still practiced, and persuading blacks to go to the polls; 2) abolishing economic inequalities and demanding an economic share.
Aims of Martin L. King: abolition of racial discrimination (see above) and inequality; extension of justice; abolition of poverty and daily humiliations of the black population; overcoming brutality of Ku Klux Klan
Aims of Malcolm X: abolition of racism, segregation, and discrimination; overcoming brutality of Ku Klux Klan; voter registration and voter education, becoming active politically; protection of civil rights workers
Aims of Amiri Baraka: the black man must get land of his own, and by doing so find his racial identity.

2.5 *Register:* emotive (frequent use of comparatives and superlatives; adjectives, verbs, and nouns arousing emotions: sincere, segregated, ugly, brutality, bombings, crisis, tension, love, extremist, enemies, hate, vicious mobs, lynch, drown, etc.)
Style: emotional (see register), concrete precise description of the black people's situation, poetic (many stylistic devices), varied (large variety of words), simple (predominantly simple sentence structure)
Speech level: between normal (neutral) and literary (formal); [cf. *MW 2*, pp. 126/127]
Stylistic devices:

a) rhetorical questions: "Was not Jesus an extremist for love?"; "Isn't this like condemning Jesus . . .?"
b) climax: "and you have to concoct . . ."; "and you are humiliated . . ."; "curse, kick, and even kill . . ."
c) alliterations: "*u*nwise and *u*ntimely"; "your *t*ongue *t*wisted and your speech *s*tammering . . ."; "*a*t *w*ill . . . *a*t *w*him", etc.
d) contrasts: "day-in and day-out"; "white" and "colored"; "by day and . . . by night"; "injustice . . . justice", etc.
e) repetitions (anaphora): "When you have seen vicious mobs . . . – when

you have seen hate-filled . . . – when you see the vast majority . . ."; "I have no despair . . ." – "I have no fear . . ."; "We will reach . . ." – "we will win . . ."

f) image: airtight cage of poverty

2.6 *Suggestion:* Have the students write letters in *English* to the publishers of *Time Magazine* and *Der Spiegel* and ask for a copy of each of the articles suggested.

The addresses: Time Magazine, Ottho Heldringstraat 5,
1066 AZ Amsterdam, The Netherlands
Spiegel Verlag, Postfach 110420,
2000 Hamburg 11

3.1 Baldwin: the whites are the blacks' *younger* brothers; they are *fearful* and therefore aggressive; being the younger brothers they are *innocent* and *unknowing,* they don't *understand;* they have wrong ideas of the blacks' inferiority and any attack on these preconceptions conjures up the danger of *their loss of identity,* which, in turn, is the main reason for their uncertainty and fear; the whites must be forced with love to *face reality.* In other words: Baldwin sees the whites as *fearful, unknowing adolescents* who must still *grow up* to face the facts of life.

June: 2003: The whites again demonstrate their *wrong preconceptions* and *ignorance:* in their opinion the "niggers" are too stupid to have rockets ("All the damn-fool things. Where'd they get rockets?"); they think there are laws to prevent the "niggers" from producing rockets ("Could they do that?" . . . "Ain't there a law?"); they believe the blacks can be bribed to stay (". . . you stay on and I raise your pay") and morally blackmailed ("Don't you love me, Lucinda?"); they don't understand the actual reasons for the blacks' emigration: the desire for freedom and a land of their own. The whites (Teece) demonstrate their mean character; the blacks are morally superior: they collect money for Belter. Like Baldwin, Bradbury depicts the whites (at least those living in the South) as unknowing children whose misconceptions are destroyed when "the order of nature" is shaken by the emigration of the blacks.

3.2 Baraka wants blacks to find their racial pride and national identity by winning land of their own. In Bradbury's short story they have achieved these aims. Racial problems are being solved by the blacks' emigration to the Mars.

14 JUNE 2003

1.1.1 List of slang expressions from text:
'em (l. 4): dropping letters: them;
them leaving (l. 5), I got to see that (l. 12), where they going? (l. 12): incomplete sentences (ellipse);
goin' (l. 24): dropping of 'g' in ing-form;
ain't (l. 33): contraction for various 'to be' forms;
I am not comin' for no . . . (l. 46): double negation;
bucks (l. 77): special expressions: dollars;
generally simple sentence structure (like the colloquial speech level!).

1.1.2 See 1.1.1

1.1.3 a) Slang: nationwide, substandard; dialect: restricted to a locality; cant: special language of underworld; jargon: restricted to particular group.

b) Foreign languages: crank = ill and grouchy
extension of meaning: bean = head
grammatical analogy: his'n: mine
invention: gimmick: = gadget
abbreviation: mike: = microphone
foreign pefixes and suffixes: sfnik
younger generation: pot: = marijuana
special groups: Harlem: cool
criminal classes: five grand;
advertising: coffee-er.

1.1.4 – –

1.1.5 The aim of these assignments is not only to work on the different speech levels, but also to show the way difficult texts can be simplified grammatically and structurally.

a) Speech levels: slang: nobody got no right, so long as he don't, ain't worth; colloquial: a damn. Tone: humorous.
We think these truths are clear to everybody; all men are created equal; they have been given by their Creator certain rights that can't be taken away from them; life, liberty and happiness are among these rights; governments are instituted among men in order to guarantee these rights; these governments must have their power from the consent of the people; whenever a government doesn't act according to these rules, it can be done away with ((exchanged for another)) and a new one can be installed ((elected)), which will care for the safety and the well-being ((interest, happiness)) of the people.

1.1.5 b) Differences:

Original	**Simplified Version**
hard words: expound, recondite	simple, easy words: explain, difficult

long, complex sentences: Our chairs, being . . . (cf. p.)	simple sentences: our chairs . . .
great deal of information	ellipses in brackets
	abridgement: dropping of information: This is how . . .

1.1.6 a) adult – grown-up, I ain't – I'm not – I am not, alien – foreigner, ameliorate – improve, amiable spouse – loving wife, as other men do – like other men do, be off – scram – buzz off – depart, bloke/guy – man, booze – drink to excess, buy – purchase, buzz off – depart, cease – stop, clad – dressed, clothe o.s. with – put on – dress, cogitate – think, con – convention – (contra), convention – con, cordial reception – hearty welcome, crazy – nuts, he died – he has had it, depart – buzz off – scram – be off, a desirable mansion – a nice house, dismiss – give s.o. the air, dough – money, dress – put on – clothe o.s. with, dressed – clad, drink to excess – booze, drunk – tight, dwell – live, excellent – smashing, five grand – $ 5000, $ 5000 – five grand, flu – influenza, foreigner – alien, fortunate individual – lucky fellow, fount – spring, give s.o. the air – dismiss, grown-up – adult, he has had it – he died, hearty welcome – cordial reception, I'm not – I ain't – I am not, improve – ameliorate, influenza – flu, like other men do – as other men do, live – dwell, loving wife – amiable spouse, lucky fellow – fortunate individual, man – bloke/guy, money – dough, nasty smell – unpleasant odour, nuts – crazy, pensive – thoughtful, peruse – read, purchase – buy, put on – dress – clothe o.s. with, rat catcher – rodent exterminator, read – peruse, rodent exterminator – rat catcher, scram – depart – be off, buzz off (the Queen would say: "I wish you would go away"!), smashing – excellent, spring – fount, stop – cease, think – cogitate, tight – drunk, thoughtful – pensive, unpleasant odour – nasty smell, if I was – if I were, whence – from where, from where – whence.

(______ = formal, - - - - = slang)

1.1.6 b)
1. less possible, because law jargon.
2. "I saw that I shouldn't get in her way."
3. versatile – all-round adaptable, contrive – think up, heretofore – up to now, blast – shoot, shrinking fragments – small pieces, honor – accept and guarantee, intact – undamaged, vastly – greatly, ascend – go up.

1.2
1. Later that night we wandered the halls of the hotel.
2. Puzzled, they drifted the big ship close.
3. She sat back on her heels by the kettle, still shining the torch at the thing.
4. But Jill did as she would not have dared to do a day earlier, stood her ground, and pointed to the window, made motions to open it.

5. He ran his finger down a list.
6. "Radiation? Did someone explode a bomb?"
7. "Good luck, Art. Please don't fail us."
8. Half a dozen ranchers blocked the way, talking weather and the price of beef.
9. Order now and we will rush you your pracel.
10. "She couldn't spell her name when she sat her G. C. E. s."
11. What do farmers grow here?
12. Come on, let's fly our kites!
13. Caesar marched his army across the Alps.
14. She stood the ladder against the tree.
15. She walked her dog every morning and evening.

2.1 – –

2.2

Whites	Blacks
shouting, crying (ll. 37, 102)	smiling (l. 105)
vicious (wink, l. 74)	
aggressive (almost strikes his wife, l. 60, cries for militia, l. 37, seizes reins, l. 62) et al.	soft-hearted and compliant (makes luncheon before leaving, l. 55, doesn't throw money, but sets is down, l. 108)
swear (damn darkie, l. 46)	
relentless (demands work for 50 $)	
slander (get off, plot, sneak out, l. 34)	just and honest (wants to pay his debt, l. 82)
unrespectful (You, Belter, come down, l. 63), Mister Way up . . ., l. 84)	respectful (sir, l. 64, bows, l. 107)
disdainful (could they do that, l. 31)	
UNSYMPATHETIC	SYMPATHETIC
NEED BLACKS	CAN DO WITHOUT WHITES

2.3 In order to arouse attention and tension.
It is appropriate. It adds to the dramatic momentum, the departure of the negroes: leaving and being left. The Belter incident constitutes the retarding moment; afterwards the tension rises afresh.

2.4 Mr Teece (Mrs Teece, Grandpa. Quartermain) – Belter.
The relationship Teece – Belter is a symbol of the relationship between Whites and Blacks in general, the two persons are not interesting as individuals, so there's no need for further names and individuals, that's why Bradbury so often uses 'someone' etc.

3.1 – –

3.2 No solution.: evasion of problem. The story might be symbolic: the negro problem can only be solved by complete separation (with the help of technology). Note: the story was written in 1950, four years before racial separation in schools was declared unconstitutional by the Supreme Court.

3.3 – –

4.1 – –

4.2 King: free from discrimination and segregation, freedom = equality.
Spiritual: free from slavery, freedom = independence.
Bradbury: free from Whites, freedom = separation.

4.3 – –

4.4 The photos were taken by W. Rumpf in the summer of 1984 on Washington's estate Mount Vernon, Virginia, near Washington D. C.

15 BLACK AMERICAN VERSE

Assignments

1. – –

2. McKay loves his country though it is hell to him, treating him badly and showing its hatred for blacks. He loves its culture, its vigour, and its bigness. These features of America, in turn, empower him to withstand America's hatred for its black citizens and make him regard the treatment of blacks as a challenge and a test he is sure to withstand. But America itself will "sink" in this struggle, a development he deplores ("Darkly I gaze . . .") because it's not only white America but the America of all races which will be destroyed by "Time's unerring hand". Angelo Lewis, on the other hand, depicts an America for which he has no sympathy, whose defeat and decline symbolize the defeat of the whites. He is even overjoyed that the America which oppresses his black brothers bleeds, that it falls, lies in the dirt, and that he can contribute to its death.

3. America's decline, predicted by Claude McKay for the future, is seen as imminent in *America Bleeds.* America is on its knees. While McKay celebrates the black man's courage and ability to face white America's hatred, Lewis appeals to his brothers finally to kill this monster. His poem provides a clear image of white America's decline. He belongs to a new generation which is not content with facing white America's hate but is determined to destroy white America.

4. Yes. The sufferings of people, their oppression by a country's majority, and their rebellion against injustice, inequality, discrimination, and brutality cannot be seen as trivial. Moreover, both deal with the future of a country, which is an important topic, too.

5.1 *America* shows a regular iambic pentameter, which results in a heavy, marching rhythm. *America Bleeds,* however, has a jerky rhythm, a breathless tempo without any regularity, because of its micro-sentences and the piling up of its impressions.

5.2 America: l. 9: run-on line; the others are end-stopped

America Bleeds: run-on lines: 1, 2, 3 (despite comma!), 6, 7, 8, 9, 10, 17 (despite comma!), 18, 25.
end-stopped: 4, 5, 11–16, 19–24

Run-on lines make the rhythm smoother and more fluent. Without the run-on lines, the rhythm of *America Bleeds* would be still jerkier than it already is.

End-stopped lines make the rhythm heavy, and structure the sentences so that sequences of words can be understood more easily.

5.3 *America's* metrical scheme:

ll. 1–5:	∪ ´ | ∪ ´ | ∪ ´ | ∪ ´ | ∪ ´ | =	iambic pentameter
l. 6:	∪ ´ | ∪ ´ | ∪ ´ | ∪ ´ | ∧ ∧ | =	4 iambic feet + pause
ll. 7–14:	iambic pentameter	

5.4 No, there isn't. It's called "free verse".

5.5 Yes, there are. The heavy marching rhythm in *America* fits the pride and strength of the speaker as well as the sombre mood resulting from America's sad destiny. Free verse, in turn, is absolutely appropriate to Lewis's passionate engagement on behalf of the liberation of his black brothers, and his appeal to them to do away with oppressive white America.

5.6 abab cdcd efef gg. Three quatrains and a rhymed couplet is typical of a *Shakespearean sonnet.*

Suggestion: After a student has given a short address about the sonnet (history, form, etc.; see assignment 6) it's perhaps worthwhile directing the students' interest to the fact that McKay has not only made use of the Shakespearean sonnet form (see p. 80) but also of the motive of "Devouring Time" which Shakespeare's sonnets often deal with (in the form, however, of "Love as the Defier of Time"). Thus, the sonnet *"America"* could serve as a jumping–off place for the study of some of Shakespeare's most famous sonnets, such as nos 15, **18,** 19, 59, 63, 106, **116, 123** (18, 116, and 123 are a "must"!).

Recommended edition of Shakespeare's sonnets:
Fischer Bücherei, Exempla Classica, 5 (with German translation)
Recommended interpretation of Shakespeare's sonnets:
J. B. Leishman, *Themes and Variations in Shakespeare's Sonnets,* Harper & Row paperback, New York.

5.7 Figures of speech used in *America:*

alliteration: *b*read of *b*itterness; *t*iger's *t*ooth; *t*ouch of *T*ime; *s*inking in the *s*and

personification: America = she; Time

metaphor: bread of bitterness; tiger's tooth; cultured hell; walls; granite wonders; touch of . . . unerring hand

simile: like tides; like a flood; as a rebel; like priceless treasures
Figures of speech used in *America Bleeds:*
alliteration: *b*leeding, *b*rothers; *c*ome . . . *c*rippled; *f*all *f*latly; *b*lood . . . *b*rothers; *d*ies . . . *d*irt; *f*low *f*reely . . . *f*all
climax: come rushing, walk crippled, fall flatly;
flow freely, move over, fall down, . . . be finished . . .
ellipsis: all of them innocents ("are" missing);
have seen it ("I" missing);
rolling in gutter ("the" missing)
metaphor: tears of sad streets; this monster; spill blood at; cough no; America bleeds (verbal metaphors)
personification: America as monster; living dreams
repetition: it does; i have seen it; etc.
symbol (emblem): red, white, & blue (for America)
synecdoche: cold eyes

5.8 No.

5.9 No. (See assignments 5.1, 5.5). It's difficult to imagine how an appeal for revolution (the dissolution of order) could be combined with a sonnet, a poem that follows a fixed structure and lays importance on a refined form.

6. **Sonnet:** A LYRIC poem of fourteen lines, highly arbitrary in form, and following one or another of several set RIME conventions. Critics of the *sonnet* have recognized varying classifications, but to all essential purposes two types only need be discussed if the student will understand that each of these two, in turn, has undergone various modifications by experimenters. The two characteristic *sonnet* types are the Italian (Petrarchan) and the English (Shakespearean). The first, the Italian form, is distinguished by its bipartite division into the OCTAVE and the SESTET: the OCTAVE consisting of a first division of eight lines riming *abba abba* and the SESTET, or second division, consisting of six lines riming *cde cde, cdc cdc,* or *cde dce.* On this twofold division of the Italian sonnet Gayley notes: "The octave bears the burden; a doubt, a problem, a reflection, a query, an historical statement, a cry of indignation or desire, a vision of the ideal. The sestet eases the load, resolves the problem or doubt, answers the query, solaces the yearning, realizes the vision." Again it might be said that the OCTAVE presents the narrative, states the proposition or raises a question; the SESTET drives home the narrative by making an abstract comment, applies the proposition, or solves the problem. So much for the strict interpretation of the Italian form; as a matter of fact English poets have varied these items greatly. The OCTAVE and SESTET division is not always kept; the RIME-SCHEME is often varied, but within limits no Italian *sonnet* properly allowing more than five RIMES: IAMBIC PENTAMETER

is essentially the METER, but here again certain poets have experimented with HEXAMETER and other METERS.

The English (Shakespearean) *sonnet,* on the other hand, is so different from the Italian (though it grew from that form) as to permit of a separate classification. Instead of the OCTAVE and SESTET divisions, this *sonnet* type characteristically embodies four divisions: three QUATRAINS (each with a RIME pattern of its own) and a rimed COUPLET. Thus the typical RIME-SCHEME for the English sonnet is *abab cdcd efef* gg. The COUPLET at the end is usually a commentary on the foregoing, an epigrammatic close. The Spenserian *sonnet* combines the Italian and the Shakespearean forms, using three QUATRAINS and a COUPLET but employing linking RIMES between the QUATRAINS, thus *abab bcbc cdcd ee.*

Certain qualities common to the *sonnet* as a type should be noted. Its definite restrictions as to form make it a challenge to the artistry of the poet and call for all the technical skill at the poet's command. The more or less set RIME patterns occurring regularly within the short space of fourteen lines afford a pleasant piquancy to the ear of the reader, and create truly musical effects. The rigidity of the form precludes a too great economy or too great prodigality of words. Emphasis is placed on exactness and perfection of expression. The brevity of the form favors concentrated expression of idea or passion.

The *sonnet* as a form developed in Italy probably in the thirteenth century. Petrarch, in the fourteenth century, raised the *sonnet* to its greatest Italian perfection and so gave it, for English readers, his own name. The form was introduced into England by Thomas Wyatt, who translated Petrarchan *sonnets* and left over thirty examples of his own in English. Surrey, an associate, shares with Wyatt the credit for introducing the form to England and is important as an early modifier of the Italian form. Gradually the Italian *sonnet* pattern (which had proved somewhat too rigid for English poets) was modified and since Shakespeare attained greatest fame for poems of this modified type his name has often been given to the English form. Among the most famous sonneteers in England have been Shakespeare, Milton, Wordsworth, and D. G. Rossetti. Longfellow, Jones Very, G. H. Boker, and E. A. Robinson are generally credited with writing some of the best *sonnets* in America. With the interest in this poetic form, certain poets following the example of Petrarch have written a series of *sonnets* linked one to the other and dealing with some unified subject. Such series are called SONNET SEQUENCES. Some of the most famous SONNET SEQUENCES in English literature are those by Shakespeare (154 in the group), Sidney's *Astrophel and Stella,* Spencer's *Amoretti,* Rossetti's *House of Life,* and Mrs. Browning's *Sonnets from the Portuguese.* William Ellery Leonard, Elinor Wylie, Edna St. Vincent Millay, and W. H. Auden have done distinguished work in the *sonnet* and the SONNET SEQUENCE in this century.

From: Thrall/Hubbard/Holman, *A Handbook to Literature,* The Odyssee Press, New York 1960, pp. 465/466.

APPLICANT

1. – –
2. Treatment of individual by larger social units, here: firm. 'Man Against Man': a human individual is destroyed by society, here in the guise of a firm.
3. He is: not listened to, disregarded, brainwashed, humiliated, not allowed to finish sentences, or to express himself.
4. Cheerful – affable – nervous – collapses.
talking – silent
standing – sitting – crawling – lying.
5. Anhänger: trailer, supporter, pendant, tag/label
Bank: bench, bank
Birne: bulb, pear
Bruch: break, crack, violation, (treaty, law), quarry (Stein-), fracture (med.), fraction (math.)
fahren: drive, ride
Geist: mind, ghost, spirit
Gericht: dish, court
Geschirr: crockery, harness
grüßen: greet (general), salute (mil.)
Hahn: cock, tap (water)
Inhalt: volume, content
Isolierung: insulation (building), isolation
Kohle: coal, dough (money)
Kreuzung: crossroads/intersection, crossbreeding
Laster: vice, truck/lorry
Lauf: barrel, run
mischen: mix, shuffle (cards)
Profil: profile, tread (tyre)
Programm: program(me), guide (tv-magazine!)
raten: guess, advise
schlagen: toll (bell), beat, whip (cream), chime (Gong), strike
scharf: hot (sauce), sharp
Schlange: queue/line, snake
Stock: stick, storey

Strom: stream, current (el.)
unterhalten: entertain, support, talk; enjoy o. s., keep a car, have a bank account
Wiederholung: repetition, re-run/repeat (tv!)
Zeche: bill, mine/pit
Zucht: discipline, breed.
arm: Arm, Waffe
blue: blau, trübsinnig/melancholisch
board: Brett, Ausschuß/Gremium, Bord (naut.)
bottom: Grund, Ende, Hosenboden
bug: Käfer/Wanze, Wanze (techn.), Fehler
cast: Wurf, (Guß)form, Besetzung (theat.), Gipsverband
check: Überprüfung/Kontrolle, Hemniss/Sperre, Scheck
degree: Grad, Maß
estate: Gut, Besitz, Stand
fan: Anhänger, Fächer
fiend: Teufel/Dämon, Fanatiker
fit: gesund, passend, angebracht
hand: Hand, Hilfe
pocket: Tasche, Gebiet/Einsprengsel
second: zweiter, Sekunde, Nachschlag
set: Satz, Gruppe, Reihe
tight: fest, betrunken, dicht, schwierig
touch: berühren, Stil, Verbindung
wet: naß, lasch, kein Alkoholverbot.

6. – –

7. Answers to "It Pays to Enrich Your Word Power"

1. **denouement** – B: A plot's unravelling; as, the *denouement* of a thriller, identifying the murderer. French *dénouer* (to unknot).
2. **lyric** – D: Words of a song; as, Oscar Hammerstein II wrote the *lyric* for the title song in *The Sound of Music.* Greek *lurikos* (lyre).
3. **auditorium** – B: Audience space; as, the Open Air Theatre at Scarborough, North Yorkshire, has a 7,000-seat *auditorium* with room for 2,000 more standing – the biggest open air theatre in Britain. Latin *audire* (to hear).
4. **mime** – C: Wordless acting or imitation; as, the silent humour of the French *mime* expert, Marcel Marceau, pretending to be a tightrope walker. Greek *mimos* (imitator).
5. **décor** – A: Scenery, stage decoration; as, the sumptuous *décor* for the ballroom scene in the ballet *Cinderella.* French *décorer* (to decorate).
6. **compère** – D: Master of ceremonies, commentator; as, Ea-

monn Andrews, *compère* of television's *This Is Your Life.* French (godfather).

7. **proscenium** – C: Part of stage in front of curtain, especially with enclosing *proscenium* arch. Greek *pro* (before) and *skene* (stage).
8. **soliloquy** – C: Speech by actor to himself; as, Hamlet's famous *soliloquy,* "To be or not to be." Latin *solus* (alone) and *loqui* (speak).
9. **aria** – A: Accompanied song for one voice, usually in opera; as, the *aria One Fine Day* in Puccini's opera, *Madam Butterfly.* Italian (air).
10. **tableau** – B: Motionless grouping of players; as, a *tableau* on a carnival float. French (picture).
11. **montage** – B: Series of film sections, cut and pieced together as a consecutive whole; as, an exciting *montage* of a car chase. French *monter* (to mount).
12. **repertoire** – D: Stock of plays; as, The National Theatre's *repertoire* of modern dramas. French.
13. **prologue** – B: Introduction, especially to a play or opera; as, a chorus speaks the *prologue* to Shakespeare's *King Henry the Fifth.* Greek *pro* (before) and *logos* (speech).
14. **encore** – D: extra performance; as, the audience applauded so loudly that the star sang an *encore.* French (again).
15. **ballerina** – A: Leading female dancer; as, after dancing *Swan Lake* in Vienna in October 1964, *ballerina* Margot Fonteyn and Rudolf Nureyev received 89 curtain calls – the world record. Italian, feminine of *ballerino* (dancing master).
16. **entr'acte** – A: Interlude, usually musical, between acts of a play. French *entre* (between) and *acte* (act).
17. **virtuoso** – C: Skilled performer; as, Julian Bream, *virtuoso* of the guitar, Italian (skilful, virtuous).
18. **choreography** – D: Arranging or designing of ballet or dance steps; as, Sir Frederick Ashton's *choreography* for the film ballet, *The Tales of Beatrix Potter* Greek *khoreia* (chorus) and *graphia* (writing).
19. **libretto** – A: Text of an opera or other long musical vocal work; as, Wagner wrote his own *libretto* for his opera *Lohengrin.* Italian (little book).
20. **matinée** – C: Afternoon performance; as, the theatre presented a *matinée* every Saturday. French *matin* (morning).

Phonetic transcription:

1) deɪ'nuːmɑ̃ːŋ
2) 'lɪrɪk
3) ɔːdɪ'tɔːrɪəm
4) maɪm
5) 'deɪkɔːʳ
6) 'kompɛəʳ
7) prəʊ'siːnɪəm
8) sə'lɪləkwɪ
9) 'ɑːrɪə
10) 'tæbləʊ
11) mɒn'tɑːʒ
12) 'repətwɑːʳ
13) 'prəʊlɒg
14) 'ɒŋkɔːʳ
15) bælə'riːnə
16) 'ɒntrækt
17) vɜːtjʊ'əʊzəʊ
18) kɒrɪ'ɒgrəfɪ
19) lɪbretəʊ
20) 'mætɪneɪ

17 UP IN ARMS OVER CRIME

Assignments

1.–4. – –

5. Take into consideration:
Soviet Union: totalitarian state, no published statistics on crime: educational purpose! (Theft rates in GDR, e.g., very high). High rate of dissenters.
South Africa: Apartheid, racial problems.
USA: Tradition of freedom, mistrust of government, easy access to weapons, great social differences, racial problems. High crime rate = price for great freedom?

6. – –

7. – –

8. – –

8.1 One evening when I was taking a walk through the park a thug suddenly stopped me, pointed his gun at me and told me that this was a stick-up and I should give him my money. I answered that I had been saving that dough to buy a plane ticket to New York City and that now I couldn't go. The thug replied that I shouldn't complain because he was doing me a big favour: crime in New York City was even worse than in our city.

8.2 One evening a young cowboy was strolling through a park. Suddenly he was stopped by a thug who pointed a gun at him and ordered him to hand over his money. The cowboy gave him all the money he had with him and said: "Actually I've been saving the money to buy a plane ticket to New York City. Now I can't go." "Never mind", the thug replied, "I'm doing you a big favour. Crime in New York City is even worse than here". He grabbed the wallet and made off.

9.1 Solution: The bookkeeper lied to the inspector when he said that he had arrived only 5 minutes before him. In that case it wouldn't have been necessary for him to park his car right beside a tree, blocking the driver's door! So he had actually arrived at a time, when many cars were parked in the street and he was only able to find that particular parking place. Pict. 1: 4 o'clock – – death of boss: 5 o'clock!

9.2 Solution a) Reiley gave himself away when he mentioned the name of his murdered brother-in-law first. By his own admission, he had at least three brothers-in-law.

Solution b) In any book, page 123 and page 124 are the opposite sides of the same page.

Attention: This is the latest news of the Goetz case:

New York won't dismiss Goetz case

NEW YORK (UPI) – Prosecutors said Tuesday there are no plans to drop attempted-murder charges against Bernhard Goetz because of a statement by a police officer indicating that the subway gunman was the object of a robbery plot.
Goetz's lawyers said they were not surprised that prosecutors refused to dismiss the charges, but added that last week's statement by the officer strengthens their case for having the court throw out the attempted-murder indictment.
Officer Peter Smith told WNBC Television that one of the four youths Goetz shot, Troy Canty, 20, said immediately after the shooting last Dec. 22 on a downtown subway train, "We were going to rob him, but he shot us first."
Smith said he and his partner, who were the first police officers on the scene, told detectives about the "confession" but were never called upon to give their statements to two grand juries investigating the case.
The officer was in the district attorney's office last week on another case when he mentioned the statement given to him by Canty. A prosecutor overheard the conversation.
Canty's lawyer, Scott Greenfield, said he "did not make that statement."
"He was not intending to nor did he take any action toward robbing Mr. Goetz," Greenfield said of the youth. "I find it incredible that there was no mention of it (the statement) in a report or verbally until almost a year later."
Detectives at the 13th precinct, which investigated the Goetz case, said they were trying to determine why Smith's statement was never brought to the attention of prosecutors.
A spokeswoman for the district attorney's office said there are no plans to drop the attempted-murder charges against Goetz in light of the new evidence.
"We're confident this case will go to trial," said spokeswoman Mary de Bourbon.

But she would not comment on speculation that Canty, who is awaiting sentencing on an unrelated robbery conviction, will be charged with lying to a grand jury. Goetz, 38, who is free on $5,000 bail, claims that he shot the four youths in selfdefense because he was afraid they would mug him. At least one of the youths asked the slim, bespectacled gunman for $5. Smith's comment was the third statement in the last month that appeared to support Goetz's contentions.

From: *The Stars and Stripes,* Dec. 12, 1985

2 Charges Dismissed in Goetz Case

By Robert D. McFadden
New York Times Service

NEW YORK – A State Supreme Court justice has dismissed charges of attempted murder and assault against Bernhard H. Goetz in the shooting of four youths who approached him demanding money on a Manhattan subway train 13 months ago. The justice, Stephen G. Crane, ruling Thursday, said he was dismissing the charges because of an error by a prosecutor who instructed the second grand jury in the case last March and because statements by two of the shooting victims before that grand jury now "strongly appear" to have been perjured. Justice Crane let stand charges of possession of dangerous weapons and reckless endangerment. These were lodged last Jan. 25 by the first grand jury, which threw out the attempted murder and assault charges. In the decision, the justice said he would permit the Manhattan district attorney, Robert M. Morgenthau, to take the unusual step of impaneling a third grand jury to hear the case, which has generated a national debate over vigilantism. Mr. Goetz shot the four youths with a pistol on Dec. 22, 1984, on a subway train in lower Manhattan. After being captured 10 days later in Concord, New Hampshire, Mr. Goetz told authorities that he had sought only to defend himself when the youths surrounded him and demanded $5. The youths, all of whom were seriously wounded, told the authorities that they had merely asked him for the $5. Justice Crane said Thursday that an assistant district attorney, Gregory L. Waples, had erred in instructing the second grand jury on the law concerning justification for self-defense. The law states that a person must retreat from a confrontation unless he "reasonably" believes that force is about to be used against him. The main error, Justice Crane said, centered on what Mr. Waples had said about the "reasonableness" of Mr. Goetz when he used deadly force to defend himself. Mr. Waples, the justice said, had neglected to state that Mr. Goetz might have "reasonably believed that unlawful physical force was about to be used against him." In addition to the prosecutor's error, Justice Crane cited statements by two of the victims as having cast doubt on the truthfulness of their testimony before the second grand jury. The case was "placed in a unique light," he said, "because of major differences between the first presentation, where the grand jury dismissed the more serious charges, and the second, where it voted to indict on those charges."

The main difference, Justice Crane said "was the testimony from the two youths," who did not testify in the first grand jury hearings. He added: "If that testimony, going to the heart of the justification defense, was perjured, as it strongly appears to have been, the integrity of the second grand jury was severely undermined."

Justice Crane said that on Nov. 27, one of the first police officers to arrive at the scene of the shootings reported that one victim, Troy Canty, had told him while still in the subway car that "we were going to rob" Mr. Goetz.

Another victim, Darrel Cabey, said in an interview in November that he and his companions had intended to rob Mr. Goetz, Justice Crane noted.

From: *International Herald Tribune,* Jan. 18/19, 1986.

18 THE SEVENTH VICTIM

1.1 a) inextricable, b) elaboration, c) bear a grudge, d) ferret out, e) annihilate, f) reluctant, g) at random, h) valid, i) drive, k) award a penalty.

1.3 ECB: Emotional Catharsis Board. AD: anno domini, BA: bachelor of Arts (university degree similar to our 'Staatsexamen'), B & B: bed and breakfast, BEM: big-eyed monster (sf jargon!), CIA: Central Intelligence Agency (secret service of the USA), DJ: discjockey, E. T. extra-terrestrial (also name and protagonist of sf-film!), FBI: Federal Bureau of Investigation (federal police force of the USA), FRG: Federal Republic of Germany (Bundesrepublik Deutschland; DDR = German Democratic Republic – GDR), GI: government issue (US soldier), L. A.: Los Angeles, MA: Master of Arts (university degree, above BA), MC: Master of Ceremonies (the Germans call him 'showmaster', a word the English language does not contain!), MCP: male chauvinist pig, MIRV: Multiple Independently-targetable Re-entry Vehicle (rocket that carries a number of warheads which hit different targets; military jargon), MP: Member of Parliament, Military Police, Machine Pistol, N.Y.C.: New York City, P.O.W.: Prisoner of War, TUC: Trade Unions Congress, TV: television, VEEP: Vice President, VRC: video cassette recorder, VIP: very important person, YMCA: Young Men's Christian Association, Xmas: Christmas.

ad: advertisement, con – pro: contra – pro, condo: condominium (Eigentumswohnung; US use), dorm: dormitory, ed.: editor, e.g.: for example (exempli gratia), ft.: foot, feet, gafia: get away from it all (sf jargon meaning escape literature), hi-fi: high fidelity (technical jargon: high quality sound-reproduction), hi-tech: high technology: electronics, computerism etc., h.p.: horse power, memo: memorandum, mike: microphone, mph: miles per hour, nuke: nuclear (weapon), ped Xing: pedestrian crossing (US use), promo: promotion (e. g. sales promotion), p.t.o.: please turn over, sci-fi: science fiction, slo-mo: slow motion (pictures, film), specs: Br.: spectacles – US: specifications, sub: submarine, sync: (US use) synchrony: to be in sync with s.b., telly: television (set), varsity: university, vs.: versus, yuppie: young urban professional: eager, career-conscious middle class people (compare 'hippie').

American specialties:

Econolodge: economic lodging, Bar-B-Q: barbeque, deli: delicatessen, LUV' EM: love them, U-PEEL-EM: you peel them, cigs: cigarettes, filet-o-fish: of, thru-nite: through night, 4: for, IOU: I owe you (Schuldschein; also Br. use), K-9 society: canine (Hund-), U-Haul: you, snax while-u-wait: snacks while you wait, UR2: you are too, TRULUV: true love. B4U: before you.

2.1 – –

2.2 story – background/setting – story.

2.3 1: Patzig (Frelaine), 2: 8th (7th), 3: lady in her late fifties (girl in her twenties), 4: manager (clerk), 5: lady (girl), 6: had already had seven kills (clerk refuses to say how many), 7: Patzig (Frelaine), 8: manager (clerk), 9: complied (said he couldn't have another draw), 10: received letter (he could only refuse, then, however, he wouldn't be allowed another victim until he had served), 11: Los Angeles (New York), 12: hated (liked), 13: couldn't refuse for a second time (he wouldn't even have been granted a second draw).

3.1 Frelaine sights the girl – she is very beautiful – he falls in love with her – doesn't shoot her – reveals himself to her – takes her home – wants to marry her – but then she shoots him – he is her tenth victim!

3.2 Aggressiveness is part of human existence, has to be channelled. Compatibility with existing laws?

3.3 Because wars constitute an opportunity for change. Then the urge for change is greater, the possibility of building something new is better. Cf. *1984, Brave New World, The Wanting Seed, Facial Justice.*

3.3 Mainly II, 1.

19 A MESSAGE FROM THE FALKLANDS

1.1 **The military:**

Arms (Waffengattungen): task force, troops

Equipment: (vehicles) aircraft, carriers, destroyer, helicopter, submarines

Forces: – –

Formations and units: crews

Military life: garrison

Navy: – –

Operations: shelling

Ranks: Navy chiefs, Admiral

The war:

Battle: air cover, attack, bloodshed, casualties, defence, fighting, killing, to reconquer, undefended

Stages: defeat, invasion, surrender, victory

Types: colonial war

1.2 1. forces; 2. task force; 3. destroyer; 4. fighting/resistance; 5. shelling/bombardment; 6. missile; 7. Helicopters/Boats; 8. casualties/victims; 9. Navy; 10. surrendered

1.3 The men are the crew of a submarine. They are awaiting death because their submarine has been hit by a depth-charge and is lying on the bottom. There is no chance of their ever reaching the surface again. The other members of the crew have already died. There is only one bullet in the gun. Thus, the four arrange for a card game whose winner is allowed to shoot himself and thus die quickly.

2.1 David's arguments against the Falklands war:

a) The war is anachronistic; it is a colonial war (in 1982!) fought over a "flag", i.e. over the possession of a small island.
b) The war is fought over a "principle" (part of Great Britain has been attacked and so the attacker must be driven out.)
c) It's disproportionate to risk the lives of 28,000 soldiers and to spend millions of pounds over a small unimportant island situated somewhere in the South Atlantic and inhabited by 1,800 people.
d) No matter what the outcome of the war, Great Britain will have to come to a political agreement with the Argentines.
e) The war destroyed a possible political agreement (Argentinian sovereignty – British administration and way of life) which Argentina was ready to accept.

2.2 Wilfred Owen says that one day wars will not be waged over the possession of territory such as colonies, i. e. over power and prestige, but "on death" itself, to save lives, i. e. medically.

Reason for its use: David wants to support his argument that the war is anachronistic.

2.3/2.4 – –

2.5 Rome. In 303, the Roman emperor Diocletian made a last attempt at destroying the Christians, whose belief in pacifism, in Jesus as the greatest emperor on earth, and in social equality (all men were created equal in the sight of God, all men possessed an immortal soul) threatened to overthrow the Roman social and economic order and thus to weaken, if not to ruin, the Roman Empire. Thus, this reference serves to put the Falkland war into a historical context: it's the "British Empire's" last attempt to demonstrate its power and maintain its existence. Like Rome's attempt this one will be doomed to failure.

2.6 The quotation from A. E. Housman serves as evidence for David's belief that every generation will make the same mistakes and must go through the same sorrowful experiences. Mankind won't learn from history.

2.7 – –

2.8 It's simply *argumentative.* He doesn't do anything except compile arguments and examples that to him underline and prove that the war is absurd. (For information on "text type" refer the students to *MW1,* pp. 48/49!)

3.1 – –

3.2 a) According to Mrs Thatcher the submarine is bound for "Negotiation Island", i. e. her policy in the Falkland crisis aims at negotiations with the Argentines, not at confrontation.

b) She wants the men in the "Commons engine room" to continue powering the submarine, i. e. she doesn't want to lose Parliament's support for her policy.

c) The men are, of course, prominent MPs. From the left:

standing (with pipe)	Tony Benn (important left winger in the Labour Party)
pedalling (row nearest to us)	Roy Jenkins (one of the founders of the S. D. P.)
	David Steel (one of the leaders of the Liberal Party)
	Michael Foot (in 1982, leader of the Labour party)
	John Silkin (Lab.)
	Denis Healey (leading member of the Labour party, right winger)
	David Owen (together with Roy Jenkins founder of the S. D. P.)
	Edward Heath (prominent member of the Conservative party; Prime Minister in the early 1970's)
on conning tower (with binoculars)	Francis Pym (in 1982, Foreign Secretary)
(with map)	John Nott (in 1982, Secretary for Defence)
(with hat)	Margaret Thatcher (P. M.)

d) Their looks show that they do not feel very happy in their role of supporting Government policy. They are either doubtful whether the Prime Minister is telling them the truth, or they support her policy because of the pressure of the public opinion.

e) Tony Benn was against Mrs Thatcher's Falklands policy from the very beginning: he is not pedalling, resp. powering the submarine; he is about to leave via the escape hatch (he appears to be wearing a life jacket!).

f) "Rejoice" (= pleasure, happiness, joy) is the ironical name for Mrs Thatcher's dangerous and bloody "voyage" to the Falklands: on one occasion, early in the war, Mrs Thatcher told the media to "rejoice" at news of a British military success.

   She claims her policy aims at peaceful negotiations (Negotiation Island!) which will make everybody happy, but in reality she is steering a very different course (see the stormy sea and the sinking ship!).

   Additional point to ponder: Why does the cartoonist show a submarine, not a destroyer or any other ship?

   Answer: Because he wants to show that those in the "engine room" have no idea what is really happening "up top". They simply follow the orders and reports relayed back to them. They are, effectively, prisoners of Mrs Thatcher like galley slaves. Another ship would possibly allow them to have a look through the portholes.

20 THE WAR OF THE WORLDS

Language 1

1. The police have cracked down on / taken strong action against the traffic of drugs.
2. She thanked him for standing up for / supporting/defending her arguments.
3. You can always fall back on / come to me for help in care you need someone.
4. I can't put up with / bear/tolerate this mess.
5. His wife was always getting on at / criticizing him for not helping with the household.
6. I don't know when I'll get around to / manage to mow(ing) the lawn.
7. He's trying to get in with / become friendly / be on good terms with his boss.
8. Damn women, he grumbled to himself, always trying to horn in on / interfere with a man's game.
9. Three new Trident subs, carrying 576 missiles, more than make up for / substitute for the loss.
10. The Coal Board averted the walkout by backing down on / reversing a decision to stop . . .
11. Scargill fell out with / quarrelled with the Communists.
12. I must read up on / increase my knowledge of English literature before the exam starts.
13. Hold on to / cling to that rope and I'll pull you up!

14. They looked down on / despised us because we didn't have a car.
15. The garrison wanted to stand out against / resist the besieging army as long as it could.

Language 2

aver, comment, content, **concern,** convert, concert, decrease, digest, **disgust,** forebear, **infer, indict,** increase, object, **presume, perfect,** prefix, produce, present, project, second, reprint, **surround,** suspect, subject, **surprise (odd men out)**

Analysis

1. Invasion from space, overcome not by man's own strength and ingenuity, but by the help of nature (God).
2. Impact of landing too great for survival; too little time passes to cover distance Mars – Earth; within one hour of radio play: eruptions on Mars, flight from Mars to Earth, defeat of the USA.
3. Flies, rats: puniness, insignificance.
4. 1: introduction (eruptions, interview with astronomer), 2: report from site, 3: speech of secretary, 4: plane fight, 5: fall of New York (climax and turning point), 6: Pierson's final notes.
5. 1) music programme interrupted with amazing news, 2) onsite reports and sound effects, 3) interview and expert commentary, 4) speech by secretary (not president who is known by everybody!), 5) public personalities and institutions: observatory, secretary of interior, astronomer, air force, 6) people "like you and me": farmer, 7) military and political action, 8) appeals to the public.
6. Cf. 'realism'! Invasion from space, appearance of aliens: what do they look like, how will they act and react?; purpose of aliens; fight against them; fight lost, but intervention of nature; retardation: occurences on Mars, but astronomer says Mars is probably not inhabited. Interruptions of music programme, switching between scenes. Escalating action: white flag, army tanks, air force, fall of New York. Fast pace: most scenes take less than one minute, it takes two minutes for Pierson and Phillips to go from Princeton to Grover's Mill!, cf. no. 2!

Discussion and Comment

1. War scare (cf. also annotations!), fear of Germany.
2. Allegory: invaders (Martians) can stand for earth-born enemies (Germany, or the Soviet Union in the film version from 1953); the relationship Martians – Earth can, of course, be applied to any inimical confrontation in which one opponent is doomed to lose: in the 1930s: Italy – Ethiopia, Germany – Spain, e.g.

Parody: *The War of the Worlds* is a seemingly realistic report on a fantastic event, a non-event, the 'suspense of disbelief' – necessary for sf – is no longer necessary because of the verisimilitude of the fantastic event.

3. Place: Great Britain – USA; time: 1898 (cf. no. 4, l. 36, no 5, l. 1 + 2) – 1938. Play: faster paced, hectic action, no broad depictions typical of novels, stronger impact and effect.

5. Ending necessary to stress meaning and message of the story: mankind is frail and fragile, must rely on help from the outside: God, chance, nature. This is also what the text menas by 'moment of truth'.

6.1 Speech, sound, music, quietness.

6.2 Difference from tv: absence of visual element.

6.3 Difference from theatre: absence of audience and their reaction, mind = stage.

6.4 a) Length: it should not be too long, radio plays mostly last 45 to 60 minutes, rarely up to 90;
b) number of characters: not too many, maybe three at the beginning, later up to eight;
c) plot and action: simple, linear, consecutive, causal, as there is no visual backing and reinforcement!;
d) exposition: short, simple, concise, maybe lasting for the first five minutes.

6.5 Action, idea, atmosphere.

6.6 Society and social criticism: frailty of society (cf. no. 5); disillusionment: Welles in introduction! (p. 172, l. 7); peace, serenity and dominion over earth short-lived; play of fantasy; invasion from Mars; didactic aim: frailty of human existence, warning against war, cosmic viewpoint: life outside the earth.

N.B.!: FINLAND

Radio Active Fallout

Snow was falling, and it was bitingly cold on the last Sunday in 1985. But for thousands of unsuspecting Finnish listeners tuned to the state radio network during the afternoon, the chilly winter day almost became too hot. Expecting some light entertainment, they instead heard "newscasters" announce that World War III had begun. The West German city of Hamburg had been pulverized by a Soviet nuclear missile, the broadcast said, while radioactive fallout was threatening Finland. Already 500 million people had perished in the first exchanges of a great nuclear confrontation.

Like *War of the Worlds,* Orson Welles' famous 1938 radio play that convinced thousands of Americans that Martians had invaded the state of New Jersey, the 2½-hour Finnish broadcast was out-and-out fiction, adapted from U. S. Playwright

Jan Hartman's prizewinning play *The Next War.* Despite warnings before, during and after the show, the broadcast sparked several hours of panic throughout the country; emergency telephone lines were jammed. "I really thought that the war had come," said Matti Korponen, a Helsinki engineer. State Radio Department Chief Mirjam Polkunen promised that no such documentaries would ever be aired again. Said she: "We didn't mean to scare anyone."

From: *TIME* 2/86

21 SOME POEMS ON WAR AND DEATH

Introducing the Topic

1. In the centre of the picture on the left we see a huge cross with the corpse of an enormous soldier nailed to it. Immediately behind the lighted cross the dark outlines of a triumphal arch are looming up. Around the gigantic cross and the triumphal arch an immense number of onlookers have gathered to watch a military parade of the kind Hitler loved to stage in his heyday.
   The right-hand drawing shows an industrialized city (New York?) floating over a field of dead soldiers lying under an endless row of cannon barrels. An aircraft is sweeping over the battle-field.
2. – –
3. Both pictures are clearly prophetic, anticipating World War II. The first drawing's message hinges on two main contrasts:
   1) *the triumphal arch:* symbol of victory of one nation over an other in war, i.e. a symbol of human hubris: the triumphal arch is built to celebrate one's own greatness and to demonstrate the enemy's humiliation. It is contrasted with the *cross:* symbol of man's sufferings, but also of man's hopes for a better world.
   2) *Onlookers* and *soldiers* celebrating the victory form an ironic and "obscene" contrast to the ghostly, gigantic martyr-soldier hanging crucified over the military parade, having died for the "sins" of mankind.
   Thus, the drawing is a protest against a world in which wars are fought and millions of lives sacrificed to gain power and superiority over other nations.
   The industrialized city, the cannon barrels and the aircraft shown in the right-hand drawing are clearly symbolic, too: all symbolize death. The city is drawn as the manifestation of technology (n.b. the turning wheels) used to produce deadly weapons. It is seen in the Expressionist tradition as a demonic power bringing death to man, as a symbol of hubris (cf. the skyscrapers), as a symbol of man's creative powers turned perverse.

Assignments

1.1 – –

1.2 Seligman's poem deals with man's sad fate here on earth, the insignificant position God has assigned to man as a tiny part of the endless universe, and the impossibility of man's finding meaning in them.
As a name gives identity to a person, a title gives identity to a piece of literature. It provides the prospective reader with an idea of what or who the "story" is about. However, only the writer or a person who knows the "story" and its message well can give the "story" an appropriate title. Seligman writes about the impossibility of understanding man's existence; he has written a poem about something he can only describe, but cannot understand: he therefore cannot name the poem.

1.3 He succeeds in doing this by clearly contrasting man's greatness and insignificance. Man, on the one hand, feels so unimportant that he doesn't even dare ask God the reason for his miserable existence. On the other hand, man is God's only creation who is able to take notice of and grasp God's existence.

1.4 While Seligman regards man as both great and insignificant, Teasedale depicts man's position in the universe and his relation to nature as completely irrelevant. If he perished nature wouldn't even notice.

1.5 Teasedale's poem refers to a normal war that does not have any effect whatsoever on the natural world. Rolfe's poem, however, depicts a war which takes place in a fictive past. In this war, normality is suspended (obviously by a supernatural power or through the use of mysterious weapons). Instead of the soldiers it is the civilians who die – either by suicide or for other unusual reasons. This war doesn't spare nature: birds, like humans, commit suicide. Eventually, with nobody alive (except for the soldiers), even war dies.

1.6 The title (ironically) and the contents reveal that Rolfe sees sf's task as one of warning man about dangers that may lurk in the future. Good sf can tell us a lot about what is ahead of us.

1.7 1. section: ll. 20–23
2. section: ll. 25–28
Rolfe's reason for including these two sections, which describe deaths that sound absurd, is that he probably wants to show the complete abnormality of this war.
Seligman's sonnet has a calm, marching rhythm and a regular rhyme pattern, both of which are appropriate to the contemplative mood, as the poem considers man's insignificance as part of the universe, his misery and sufferings here on earth, his singularity as *homo sapiens.* Teasedale's poem shows frequent anapaestic feet interrupted by some iambic feet,

2.1

<table>
<tr><th></th><th>Untitled Sonnet</th><th>There Will Come Soft Rains</th><th>A Poem To Delight . . .</th></tr>
<tr><td>1. Meter</td><td>Twelve lines show regular iambic pentameter. However, lines 1 and 9 create difficulty in scanning: they have 11, not 10 syllables. It's idle to discuss whether this was intended by the poet or is simply a flaw.
Compare:
l. 1:
∪ –́ | ∪ –́ | –́ | ∪ –́ | ∪ –́ |
Not ours to ask why, when we are done
l. 2:
∪ –́ | ∪ –́ | ∪ –́ | ∪ –́ | ∪ –́ |
The litt le time we spent before the sun
l. 9:
∪ –́ | ∪ –́ | –́ | ∪ –́ | ∪ –́ |
Not ours to ask why, of end less time</td><td>The poem shows varying line lengths and metric feet. Only line 2 has regular iambic pentameter, the other lines are shorter (tetrameter); iambic and anapaestic feet alternate:
l. 1:
∪ ∪ –́ | ∪ –́ | ∪ ∪ –́ | ∪ ∪ –́ |
l. 2:
∪ –́ | ∪ –́ | ∪ –́ | ∪ –́ | ∪ –́ |
l. 3:
∪ –́ | ∪ ∪ –́ | ∧ –́ | ∪ ∪ –́ |
etc.</td><td>free verse</td></tr>
<tr><td>2. Rhythm</td><td>"marching"</td><td>more "dancing" than "marching"</td><td>free rhythm</td></tr>
<tr><td>3. Rhyme</td><td>end-rhyme (cf. MW 2, p. 136); the lines are rhymed with the exception of lines 5 and 9. "Dumb" and "from" in lines 13/14 are half rhymes (even in American English).
rhyme scheme:
aabbcdadefgfhh</td><td>end-rhyme. The rhyme in ll. 11/12 is acceptable because Americans usually pronounce "gone" as [gɔːn]

aabbccddeeff</td><td></td></tr>
</table>

	Untitled Sonnet	*There Will Come Soft Rains*	*A Poem To Delight . . .*
4. Diction	simple words; hardly any figures of speech; some alliterations; some repetitions.	simple words; one metaphor; personification (Spring); some alliterations; some anaphora; one synaesthesia (shimmering sound)	rather complicated words; many figures of speech; two metaphors (battalions, aerial radar); some similes: ponds, wounded animals, drunken stars, etc.); some repetitions (That was the year, etc.)
5. Sentence Structure	predominantly simple	partly simple, partly complex	partly simple, partly complex

which confers on the poem a more lively rhythm that fits the poem's message: after the extinction of mankind nature will continue to exist as serenely and lightheartedly as ever.

Free verse, in its turn, is particularly appropriate to Rolfe's description of the war's abnormal and horrible incidents. It produces a more powerful and dynamic drive than refined rhythmic patterns and rhyme schemes.

2.2/3 All three poems make use of alliteration. Teasedale, moreover, applies one *internal* rhyme (wear/their). Their effect is to put more stress on specific words and to contribute to the beauty of the poem.

The relatively simple diction and sentence structure of the first two poems underline the simplicity of the contents. On the other hand, the more complicated language used in Rolfe's poem corresponds to the greater complexity of the events depicted.

2.4 See also 2.1. Their effect is to embellish the language and thus to increase the reader's aesthetic pleasure.

3. **Further Studies**

3.1 Seligman's cosmology: God -- creator of the universe; creation out of nothing; extension of the universe through God; our world is transitory, the sun a dying one. Man -- the only intelligent being beside God in the universe.

Modern science: beginning: big bang (a gigantic ex[im]plosion); since then the cosmos has been expanding (Hubble effect, 1924). Two models of the future of the universe:

1) the closed model: gravity of the universe's matter causes a slow-down of the expansion and an eventual collapse of the universe, which, in turn, will result in a new big bang, i. e. the creation of a new universe, etc. This model is favoured by Marxism: matter is eternal!
2) the open model (favoured by the Catholic church): gravity is not strong enough to prevent the galaxies drifting apart. The universe continues to expand forever and "the lights will go out slowly but steadily" until there are no atoms left. This model is favoured by modern (Western) science at present.

3.2 The student should discover that

a) Bradbury's *There Will Come Soft Rains* depicts a world as it is anticipated in Teasedale's poem: mankind has been annihilated in war.
b) Teasedale's poem shows nature continuing undisturbed by war. Not so Bradbury's short story. Nature dies a slow death (the dog dies, the tree bough is torn off by the storm).
c) In Bradbury's story, technology survives longest. One house has escaped the nuclear catastrophe and goes on "living" until fire puts an end to its existence.
d) Teasedale's poem serves 1) as a re-enforcement of the story's

message: mankind is in danger of "perishing utterly" in a possible (nuclear) war in the future; 2) as an ironic contrast. A future war will not spare *any* life. Teasedale's vision is ridiculously harmless when compared with the possible holocaust caused by a nuclear war.

22 HIROSHIMA

1.1 a) He took four or five steps (l. 8) = Er machte vier oder fünf Schritte
b) . . . making one of the thousands of dugouts (l. 16) = und einen der Tausende von Unterständen machten

1.2 a) prepare; b) doing; c) take; d) go on; e) make/earn; f) pay; g) had; h) put

1.3 to give trouble = Schwierigkeiten machen
The bill comes to 20 pounds = Die Rechnung macht 20 Pfund

1.4 to make a speech; to do a test; to do business; to do wrong; to make music; to make fun of; to do a favour; to do one's best; to do one's hair; to do mathematics; to make a row; to make faces; to do the room; to make the bed; to make peace; to do well; to make a mess; to do the task; to make a choice

1.5 Some examples: a) In order to be admitted to the university he had to do a test. b) Would you do me a favour? c) When she had made the bed, mother did the room. d) Which do you prefer, doing mathematics or doing Greek? e) If you want to have your hair done you must go to a hair-dresser. f) What a mess these hooligans have made! g) Make love – Not war! h) It's impolite to make faces.

1.6 1. deceive; 2. achievement; 3. ceiling; 4. local; 5. flash; 6. dugout; 7. cloud; 8. unload; 9. clothing; 10. issue; 11. blaze; 12. splinter; 13. fragment; 14. bomb; 15. atomic; 16. respond
Solution: Chicago – Los Alamos
Chicago: First nuclear chain reaction generated by E. Fermi and his team (see assignment 3.2)
Los Alamos: Actually not a city, but a town in New Mexico; place where R. Oppenheimer and his team built the first atomic bomb.

2.1.1 At the moment when the bomb was dropped Mr Tanimoto 1. was in a suburb of Hiroshima, far enough away from the epicentre, 2. threw himself behind two rocks in the garden which protected him against the blast.

2.1.2 1. the rich man's house was destroyed, houses nearby were burning; 2. clouds of dust were everywhere producing a sort of twilight and darkening the sky over the whole of Hiroshima; 3. drops of water of unusual size began to fall
His reaction: he panicked

2.1.3 Most people were terribly burnt and in great pain; many were naked and on their bodies were printed the patterns they had had on their clothes; some were vomiting while walking. The people were all in shock; nobody spoke; none showed any expression whatsoever.

2.1.4 The hospital was totally overcrowded by casualties; ceilings and walls had come down; the electricity was cut off; few nurses and doctors had survived the explosion; only the worst cases could be treated; there was a lack of medication; corpses were lying everywhere; there weren't any helpers to carry them away.

2.1.5 The hospital staff had to work like slaves. Dr Sasaki, for example, worked for nineteen straight hours, took a one-hour nap, then went back to work.

2.2 a) Exact specifications about:

1. the times: 8.15 a. m on August 6, 1945, Japanese time and the evening of the same day
2. the places: Koi, Hiroshima, and the Red Cross Hospital
3. the events (see above)

b/c) sense units: ll. 1–10: the Explosion of the Atomic Bomb
ll. 12–30: Mr Tanimoto's First Impressions of the Bomb's Immediate Effects
ll. 33–54: The Physical and Psychic Conditions of the Population Immediately after the Bomb
ll. 61–82: The Situation in the Red Cross Hospital

d) linear, clear, logical, closed (all three extracts from Hersey's account have precise beginnings and short but effective endings.)

e/f) No. The author remains objective throughout the text. This can be clearly seen from the sober language he uses. He is eager to avoid any adjectives that arouse feelings; where they are used (e.g. "terrible", "compelling"; "complaining") he applies them because they are necessary to show what the reality was like. The same is true with the verbs and nouns. He avoids expressive verbs; verbs and nouns only mirror the facts. They are simple and concrete, without difficult words. Of course, the text impresses and touches the reader. But this is not because of the style but because of the events depicted.
The sentence structure is partly simple, partly complex. There are no compound sentences. The tense is straight past tense, which is not surprising since the type of the text is narrative.

g) Time, place, development of events: precise specifications
Persons: mentioned, but no characterization (the fact that Mr Tanimoto feels pity for the victims doesn't tell us much about his character. It's quite obvious that any human would show such feelings when confronted with such misery. He would be inhuman if he did not.)
Attitude of the narrator: objective

Language and style: sober, simple, concrete words, no descriptive adjectives, no expressive verbs and nouns, no rhetorical figures;
sentence structure: no compound sentences
tense: Past Tense

Text type: narrative

3.2/3 There are two sides and two points of view confronting each other. On the one side there are scientists like Mr Sachs who emphasise the freedom of the scientist to do research in order to unveil the secrets of nature. The application of his findings is not his business. This is the task of political groups in this society. Moreover, such scientists say, most findings can be applied in a positive and a negative way, resp. have positive and negative consequences: nuclear technology or gene technology, computers and robots, communication systems etc. can be used in wars; even the invention of the car has its bad side.

The other side emphasises that the consequences of research in specific fields may be so terrible that scientists must be controlled by political groups; the possible positive and negative consequences should be carefully considered; experiments should be stopped if the negative aspects outweigh the positive ones.

The problem, however, is that such a decision must often depend on the decision-makers' political standpoint; that the decision-makers often do not understand the scientific issues; that the complete range of positive or negative consequences cannot be always foreseen at a stage when the experiments can still be stopped.

Grammar

Simple Form – Progressive Form

1. Most verbs in our text have been used in the *Simple Past.* Can you explain why?
2. On the other hand, there are 10 examples of *Progressive Form* in the text. Find them and explain their application.
3. Insert the correct verb form in the blanks. Decide whether Simple Form or Progressive Form should be used and justify your choice.
   a) On August 9th Mr Tanimoto, who _______ (still-work / Past Tense) in Asano Park _______ (go/Past) to the suburb of Ushida, where his wife _______ (stay/Past) with friends.
   b) He _______ (get/Past) a tent, _______ (take/Past) it to the park and _______ (set/Past) it up as a shelter for some of the wounded.
   c) Whatever he did in the park, he felt he _______ (be watched/Past) by Mrs Kamai with her dead baby daughter in her arms.
   d) She kept the small corpse in her arms for four days, even though it _______ (begin/Past) smelling bad on the second day.

e) She told him that the bomb _______ (bury/Past Perfect) her under their house with the baby strapped to her back and that when she _______ (dig/Past Perf.) herself free, she had discovered that the baby _______ (choke/Past), its mouth full of dirt.
f) She _______ (clean/Past Perf.) the infant's mouth carefully, and for a time the child _______ (breathe/Past Perf.) normally but suddenly it _______ (die/Past Perf.)
g) Mrs Kamai also _______ (urge/Past) Mr Tanimoto to search for her husband.
h) He _______ (know/Past) it would be impossible to find Kamai, even if he _______ (live/Past).
i) Every time she _______ (see/Past) Mr Tanimoto, she inquired about her husband so that Mr Tanimoto began to keep away from her, but whenever he _______ (look/Past) at her, she _______ (stare/Past) at him and her eyes _______ (ask/Past) the same question.

Solution

1. The text is narrative, i.e. many actions follow each other (question: what happened then?). If this is the case the *Simple Form* must be used.
2. a) l. 15: who had been burrowing (expresses an activity that began in the past, before the time of speaking, and continued up to that time)
   b) l. 17: blood was running (action that continued for some time in the past but whose exact limits are not known and not important)
   c) l. 25: Hiroshima . . . was giving off (see b)
   d) l. 28: Houses nearby were burning (see b)
   e) l. 29: they must be coming (see b)
   f) l. 35: hundreds who were fleeing (see b)
   g) l. 38: some were vomiting (see b)
   h) l. 62: was moving (see b)
   i) l. 64: were putting (see b)
   j) l. 70: patients were dying (see b)
3. a) who *was still working* (action that began at some point in the past and continued for some time in the past but whose exact limits are not known and not important) – – *went* (Simple Past is used for a past action when the time is given) – – *was staying* (see above)
   b) *got* (action succeeds "went"; answers to the question: what happened then? – – *took* (successive action) – – *set* (successive action)
   c) he *was being watched* (see a)
   d) it *began* (see b)
   e) *had buried* (Past Perfect used when from a certain point in the past the narrator looks back on an earlier action) – – *had dug* – – *was choking* (the second action continued when the first ended)

f) *had cleaned* -- *had breathed* -- *had died* (successive actions that happened at a time earlier than that from which the narrator looks back)
g) *urged* (action succeeding "she told")
h) knew ("to know" is a verb of thinking that is not normally used in the progressive form) -- were/was living (see a)
i) *saw* (a verb of the senses is not normally used in the progressive form) -- whenever he *looked at* (action that is repeated is normally expressed by the simple form) -- *she was staring* (see a) -- *asked* (repeated action) or *were asking* (see a).

23 THAT ONLY A MOTHER

1.1 *National:* nation, nationalism, nationalist, nationality, nationalize; *tension:* tense, tenseness (= tensity), tensile (of tension, capable of being streched), intent, intensive, intensify, intense, detention (detain a pupil in school after ordinary hours, as a punishment); *immemorial:* memory, memorize, memo (randum), memento, memoirs, memorable, memorial; *familiarity:* family, familiar, familiarize.

1.2 writhe, wriggle, muscle, comb, scent.

1.3 a) watch, observe; b) she looked at him intently in order to recognize him and see if she could remember his features; c) He laughed in such a way as to keep her at a distance; d) out of proportion, on a scale larger than usual; e) gradually became quieter and quieter; f) rushed to/for.

1.4 *Anaphora:* new dress, new shoes, new slip . . . (l. 5); so many days, so many months, so many things (l. 27); the same high-bridged nose . . . the same long jaw . . . the same . . . month (l. 30).
Epiphora: traveled down . . . traveled down . . . and straight down . . . (l. 79); the soft-skinned body . . . the sinuous body (l. 97); I didn't know . . . she didn't know (l. 95 + 96).
Alliteration: last light brush-on of lip paste (l. 21); she dashed for the door (l. 22); fine feathery brows (l. 30); the baby on the big bed (l. 54); relieved laughter (l. 63).
Figura etymologica: mutations – mutants (l. 12/13); strange – stranger (l. 32/33); heard – hearing (l. 50); this baby – this baby's father (l. 63 + 65).
Metaphor: the finger of memory (l. 29).
Synecdoche/personification: sleepy lids pulled back (l. 46); his hand touched (etc.) (l. 75, 79, 84, 96); the head advanced (l. 65).

1.5 a) being nosey, b) keeping your nose to the grindstone, c) you've got your nose up in the air, d) nose out of joint, e) on the nose, f) to be led by the nose, g) a blue nose, h) to nose out your opponent.

2 Analysis

a) 1st: she is mentally advanced: she can speak and sing at the age of 10 months; 2nd: she is physically disabled: she has no limbs.

b) . . . because many babies were born disfigured.

c) . . . such a disproportionate increase the number of disfigured and mutated babies might have been avoided.

d) . . . because she wants to reassure herself and because she believes it.

e) 1st: she wants to open the knot of the baby's nightie instead of her husband; 2nd: she wants to make her baby sing when her husband is about to discover the truth; 3rd: she thinks her baby is wet when her husband has found that s.th. is wrong with the baby. . . . as psychologically defective: she represses the truth.

f) . . . speak?

g) 1: The baby crawls before turning over, 2: she looks like a potato-sack racer when propelling herself across the bed; 3: she wriggles like a worm when he gropes for an arm; 4: he doesn't feel any kicking when groping for legs.

h) . . . legs.

i) . . . that her baby is disfigured (has no limbs).

k) . . . we aren't told what Hank does (to the baby? to his wife?).

3 Discussion and Comment

3.1 World War II and the dropping of the nuclear bombs an Hiroshima and Nagasaki triggered off the author's imagination

3.2 A man would probably not have concentrated on a mother's and her baby's fate.

3.3 Of course, "building again" implies the notion of building a better society, one that has learnt from our mistakes. But isn't the only thing we learn from history the fact that we don't learn anything from it? Does history proceed along a (rising) line or does it follow a circle (of even many circles?)

3.4

Mother	The Choice	Hiroshima
nuclear war	nuclear war	nuclear war
short story	poem	account
individual fate	mankind's fate	group fate
fiction	fiction	fact
mutation	complete destruction	partial destruction
not many details	general statement	many details
psychological study	anthropological statement	factual account

3.5 She wants to drive home her argument by concentrating on the fate of a baby and parents, which might be more moving.

The consequences of such a war would be so horrible that details of it would not be relevant. Furthermore, they would break the frame of the story and add divergent threads to a tightly knit plot, thus spoiling a uniform impression.

3.6 This humorous, macabre story is about the last survivor on earth after a (nuclear?) catastrophe. As no fellow beings are left he doesn't want to go on living alone and decides to commit suicide by jumping from a top-floor window of a sky-scraper. When, while falling, he hears a telephone ring, he realizes that somebody else is still alive too, and so, of course, he regrets his decision. (Cf. also vol. III, note on *The Answer!*)

III ADDITIONAL TEXTS

"I thought I could test myself here. But I've practically reinvented myself."

SP4 Michelle Kowalski, Signal Intelligence

"I wanted a challenge in life, and I felt that the Army offered one. I knew it was going to be tough. But it was a way that I could prepare myself for the future. An inner journey to my independence.

"Like Basic Training. You're ready to break, but somehow you pull through. The Army really knows how to build you up to take stress. Training for my job in Military Intelligence also was hard. It has given me self-discipline; you're expected to be on time, responsible, versatile. My job is terrifically rewarding and exciting. Something you could never experience anywhere else.

"If you want to grow up—all the way up—and find out what you're made of, I recommend the Army. In fact, I would even say I think it's something everyone should go through."

For more information about Army opportunities, see your local Army Recruiter or call toll free 1-800-USA-ARMY.

ARMY. BE ALL YOU CAN BE.

Source: *Discover,* Oct. 1985.

Assignments

1. What is the subject of this ad?
2. The general purpose of ads has been expressed in the formula of "AIDA" (= ATTENTION; INTEREST; DESIRE; ACTION). Would you say that our ad fulfils these aims? If so, how? (To do this task consider a) what parts the ad consists of, b) which purpose each part serves, c) what group of addressees the copywriters have in mind, d) what tricks the copywriters use to achieve their intended purposes, e) which words in the text are most effective in achieving the intended purposes, f) what these words appeal to, g) what the text's style is like, and why.)
3. What effect does the ad have on *you*?

CHRISTIANE'S MOTHER

On the Sunday that I found the bloodstains in the bathroom and examined Christiane's arms, the penny really dropped. It was a severe blow. Christiane presented me, as it were, with the receipt for her education of which I had been so proud. Now I saw: I had done everything wrong, for the sole reason of not wanting to repeat the mistakes my father had made in my education.

For instance, when Christiane began to go to the Sound discotheque, I was not exactly overjoyed, but then her friend Kessi and other young people from Centre House went regularly to the Sound. I said to myself, oh, all right, why shouldn't Christiane go there now and again? All the young people raved about the Sound. I had to think of all the harmless pleasures my father forbade me when I was a girl.

I continued with this liberal upbringing when Christiane introduced her boyfriend Detlef, whom she had met in the Sound. Detlef made a very good impression on me. He knew how to behave, had good manners and an open nature. All in all, a likeable fellow. And I considered it perfectly natural for Christiane at her age to have fallen in love for the first time. I thought the main thing is that he's a decent boy. I could see that he was really fond of Christiane.

If at that time anyone had told me that these two were even then injecting heroin, I would have said he was mad. For, apart from her crush on Detlef, nothing about Christiane struck me as in any way unusual. On the contrary, she seemed to me to be calmer and more balanced after she had been for some time exceedingly rebellious. Even at school things appeared to improve.

After school we always talked to each other on the phone, and she would tell me what she was doing. That she would be going to a school friend's house or fetching Detlef from work. I had no objections. As a rule, on weekdays, she was at home for the evening meal. And whenever she was late she rang up and was home an hour later. Sometimes she went out again to Centre House or met her friends, as she said.

She began helping around the house again, and I would show my appreciation by giving her a small present, a record perhaps or extra pocket money. My boyfriend Klaus did not approve. He thought I ought to think of myself for a change. Christiane was only going to take advantage of me. In a certain sense he may have been right. But then I always had this feeling of having to do something special for Christiane, to make up to her for something. However, in those days I wasn't yet able to see this quite accurately.

My boyfriend objected to my allowing Christiane to stay with her friends overnight. He didn't believe her; he didn't believe she was really staying with a friend. But spying on her – that was not my way. That was what my father used to do to me without my ever having done anything wrong.

One day Christiane told me that she had slept with Detlef. 'Mummy, darling,' she said, 'he was so sweet to me, you can't imagine.' Now I thought I knew why she always wanted to stay with her friends at the weekend.

But it had happened. And I couldn't really see anything wrong in it. From now on I occasionally gave her permission to stay overnight with Detlef.

How could I have prevented these two from going to bed together? On TV and in the papers psychologists keep emphasising that the young people of today mature earlier and that sexuality must not be repressed. I share this view.

At least Christiane had a steady boyfriend. Other girls in our neighbourhood just slept around. For this reason alone Christiane's steady relationship with Detlef reassured me.

On the other hand, if I am quite honest, I did at times feel uneasy. Above all on account of Christiane's new friends of both sexes whom she had met in the Sound. She told me that some of them were on drugs.

She didn't mention heroin, but they smoked hash and went on trips. She described horrendous things to me, including that her friend Babsi was also a drug addict. But she talked of these things in so disgusted a tone, she found them so revolting – I should never have thought it possible that she was doing all this herself.

When I asked her: 'Why do you bother with these people?' she said: 'But, mummy, I feel so sorry for them. Nobody wants to have anything to do with them. And they're so pleased if I speak to them. They do need help.' And Christiane has always been ready to help. Today I know that she was talking about herself.

And one evening, half-way through the week, when she had not come home until eleven, she said: 'Don't be cross, mummy. I was at a release centre with the people.' And I asked: 'What goes on there?' 'Well, we talk and try to get them off drugs!' And then she added: 'If I should ever become an addict . . .' and giggled. I gave her a horrified look. Until she said: 'Well, I'm only saying that. I'm okay.' 'And Detlef?' I asked. Christiane was quite outraged. 'That's quite out of the question for Detlef. It would be the end.'

That was in the winter of '76. From then on I had a premonition, but I suppressed it. Nor did I listen to my boyfriend. By then he was willing to take any bet that

Christiane was on drugs. But I wouldn't allow him to say anything against her. One isn't all that ready to admit to oneself that it has all been in vain, that one has failed as a mother. I persisted in believing that my daughter wouldn't do that.

I tried to put Christiane on a short rein. But when I told her: 'Be back by supper time,' she just didn't come back. And then there was nothing I could do. Where was I to look for her in this city? Even without my powers of self-deception I wouldn't have suspected her on Zoo station. I was glad when she phoned at half past eight saying: 'Mummy, I'll be home soon, don't worry.' I could simply no longer cope with Christiane.

There were times, though, when she did as she was told. Then she told her friends on the phone almost proudly: 'No, I'm not allowed to go out today. I'll have to stay in.' She did not seem to mind in the least. This was the contradictory aspect of Christiane. On the one hand, she was wayward, cheeky and wouldn't listen to a word one said to her. On the other hand, she seemed to respect me when I drew clear lines. However, it was already too late.

It was towards the end of January, 1977, on a Sunday, when my moment of truth came. It was terrible. I wanted to go to the bathroom. It was locked. This was not usual in our family. Christiane was in there and wouldn't open the door. At this moment I was certain. It was clear to me, for the first time, that all this while I had been fooling myself. Otherwise I couldn't have known all of a sudden what was happening in the bathroom.

I began to bang against the door. But she wouldn't open up. I nearly hit the roof. I scolded, I begged her to open the door. At last she dashed past me. In the bathroom I found a black spoon and splashes of blood on the wall. There was my confirmation. I knew it from reports in the papers. My boyfriend said: 'Well, do you believe it now?' I ran after her into her room. I said: 'Christiane, what have you done?' I was completely at the end of my tether. I trembled all over. I didn't know whether to burst into tears or scream at her. But I had to talk to her first. She was sobbing her heart out and didn't want to look at me. I asked: 'Did you inject yourself with heroin?' She did not answer. She was weeping so bitterly that she couldn't speak. I forced her arms straight and saw the mess. She had already got needle marks on both arms. However, it didn't look too bad. Not at all. There was nothing bruised, and all one could see were two or three marks, one of them the fresh one. This one was still rather red.

And then she admitted it. Amid tears. At this moment I thought: 'I shall die.' I think I should have liked to die, too. I was so desperate that I simply couldn't think. I didn't know what to do. Then I said: 'What are we going to do?' That is what I actually asked Christiane. I myself was completely helpless.

So this was the blow I had tried to dodge. This was what I kept sweeping under the carpet. But then I didn't know how the symptoms would manifest themselves. So far I had not noticed anything languid about Christiane, nothing of the sort. Most of the time she was bright and cheerful. The only thing which had struck me during

the past few weeks was that occasionally, when she came home a little late, she disappeared into her room rather quickly. I put it down to a bad conscience. On account of being late.
After I had calmed down a little we considered what we might do. And then Christiane admitted that Detlef was also a drug addict. Any withdrawal would be pointless, she said, unless Detlef would withdraw at the same time. Otherwise they would tempt each other again and again. This seemed to make sense to me. We decided that the two of them were to start withdrawing immediately at our house.
Christiane struck me as perfectly open and honest. She also confessed to me that Detlef was earning the money for heroin by working as a male prostitute on Zoo station. I was horrified. That she solicited men herself for that very reason was never even mentioned. I did not suspect her either; after all, she loved Detlef. And he, she said, had always earned enought money for heroin. Over and over again Christiane declared solemnly: 'Mummy, believe me, I want to come off H. Really.'
That evening we started out in search of Detlef. And it was then that, for the first time consciously, I saw the emaciated pitiable creatures walking up and down between the tube trains. And Christiane said: 'I don't want to end up like them. Just look at these fucked-up guys.' She herself did still look comparatively decent. And I was almost reassured again.
We failed to find Detlef and therefore went to see his father. He knew all about Detlef's heroin addiction, but not that Christiane was an addict, too. I remonstrated with him. 'Why,' I asked him, 'didn't you tell me anything?' Because he was ashamed, he said.
Detlef's father seemed relieved. He wanted to help financially, he said. Up till now he had tried in vain to get help for his son. I must have seemed liked an angel. And I must say I felt quite strong myself. I had not the foggiest idea what was in store for me.
Next day I went off on my own looking for advice. At first I went to the youth welfare office and said: 'My 14-year-old daughter is a heroin addict. What am I to do?' They did not know. 'Put her in a home,' they suggested. I said that was quite out of the question. Christiane would have felt rejected. Besides they didn't know of a home. They would have to choose one; that would take quite a long time. In any case, good places for educationally subnormal children were few and far between. I said: 'It has nothing to do with that, she is not educationally subnormal. She's a drug addict.' They just kept looking at me and shrugging their shoulders. In the end they suggested that I should take Christiane to the child guidance clinic. When I suggested this to Christiane, she just said: 'Rubbish, what's the use, they haven't a clue. What I need is therapy.' But the authorities had nothing of that sort to offer. I went from one drug advice bureau to the other, at the Polytechnik, at Caritas, and heaven only knows where else. I did not know how to handle the problem.
The various counsellors did not hold out much hope for the success of withdrawal at home. Without therapy, they said, withdrawal was rather pointless. But Christiane was still so young I might try my luck at home. They didn't have a therapy place

available now, anyway. In three months' time, perhaps. They gave me advice on diet in case of deficiency symptoms.

The withdrawal took place during the first week. Neither of the two tried any tricks, nor did they want to clear out. My hopes rose again. After a week I was certain: Thank God, she's done it. Presently Christiane went back to regular attendance at school, where she is supposed to have taken an active part in the lessons.

But then Christiane began to hang out with the old crowd again. At least she told me every time where she was. She made unassailable statements. When she rang up at 8 pm, she said: 'Mummy, I'm in this or that café. I've met this or that person. I'll be home quite soon.'

By now I was warned. I checked her arms but could see no new punctures. She was no longer allowed to stay at Detlef's over the weekend. On the other hand, I wanted to show her that I trusted her. That's why I allowed her to stay out late on Saturday night. I was suspicious, but I simply didn't know how I was to act. I racked my brains.

From: *"H" Autobiography of a Child Prostitute and Heroin Addict,* Corgi Books, Transworld Publishers Ltd., London

Assignments

1. Why – do you think – did Christiane start taking drugs?
2. Was it her mother's fault? Were her mother's educational concepts wrong?
3. What could she have done to prevent Christiane from becoming a drug addict?
4. Would you say it's more difficult for parents to educate children today than it used to be, 20 or 30 years ago? Give reasons.
5. One student reads the book and makes a speech to the class summing up Christiane's further experiences as a drug addict.

Suggestion: Following the summary, the teacher should ask the students whether they know what Christiane ist doing today. In the event of nobody knowing, he/she should point out that the newspapers reported in November 1985 that Christiane had been apprehended by the police and drugs been found on her.

Mount Vernon – Home of George Washington

1. **Entrance Gate**
2. **Bowling Green** – Developed by George Washington in 1785. A few of the larger trees bordering the serpentine walks survive from the original planting.
3. **Gardener's House** – Records indicate that this building was used from time to time by the gardener, the shoemaker and the tailor. A part of the building may also have been used to accommodate the sick. The building is not open for exhibition.
4. **Office** – Records indicate a sequence of uses for this building: servants' hall, guest house manger's residence and office.
5. **Mansion** – In 1757/58 George

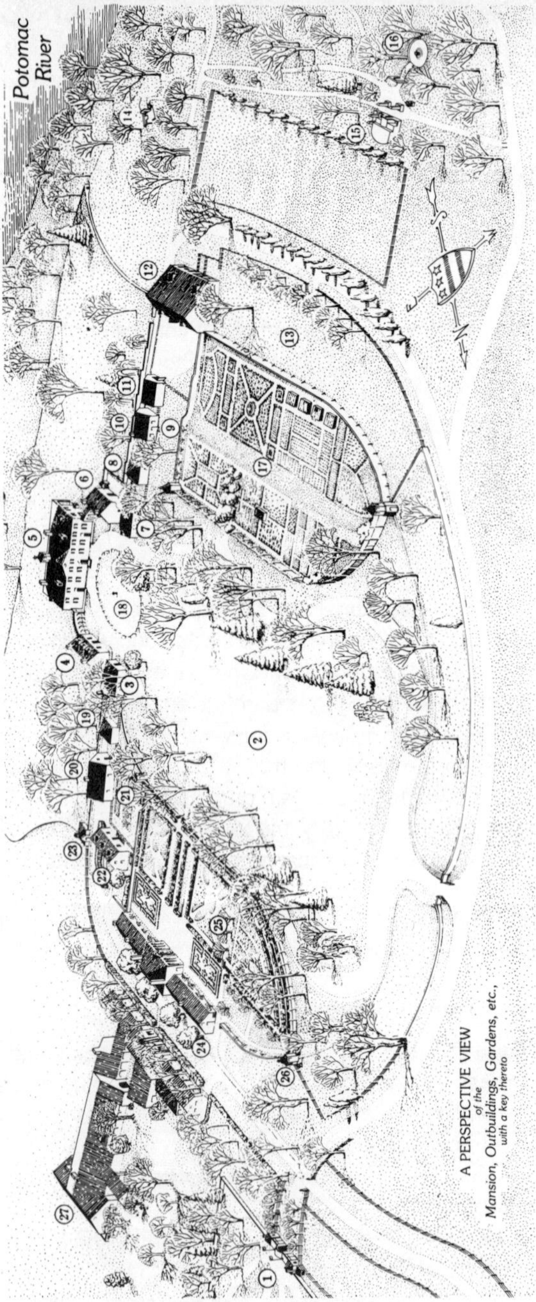
Potomac River
A PERSPECTIVE VIEW of the Mansion, Outbuildings, Gardens, etc., with a key thereto

Washington repaired and enlarged the structure from one and one-half to two and one-half stories. Shortly before the Revolution, he made plans for additions at each end of the house. The Mansion was completed in 1787.

6. **Kitchen** – Equipped with utensils and furnishings, some original to Mount Vernon, which show the wide range of open hearth cooking.
7. **Storehouse and Overseer's Quarters** – Tools and equipment were distributed from the storeroom facing the courtyard and a careful record kept.
8. **Smokehouse** – Game, hams and other meats were dried and smoked in this building close by the kitchen.
9. **Laundry Yard** – The laundry was dried and sun bleached in this space.
10. **Washhouse** – Here the family's laundry was washed and ironed.
11. **Coachhouse** – Rebuilt on the original site in 1893. An eight-eenth century riding chair is on display.
12. **Stable** – Built in 1782. The center section houses a rare American eighteenth century crane neck coach owned by the Powel family of Philadelphia, close friends of George and Martha Washington.
13. **Paddock** – An area where the numerous Mount Vernon horses and other livestock would have been temporarily confined.
14. **Old Family Vault** – Original burial place of George Washington.
15. **Tomb of George and Martha Washington** – Built in 1831–1837 by the executors of General Washington's estate, the tomb is also the burial place for about 25 other family members.
16. **Slave Burial Ground** – Site of a cemetery for many of the slaves of the Washington family.
17. **Lower Garden** – Restored within the original enclosing walls in a manner true to the time of General Washington.
18. **Courtyard** – The dial post supports the original sundial.
19. **Salt House** – Used for storage of salt for preserving and curing fish and meat.
20. **Spinning House and Slave Quarters** – A number of people were regularly employed in textile crafts at Mount Vernon.
21. **Botanical Garden** – Used by General Washington for experimental planting.
22. **Museum** – Built in 1928. Public restrooms are located under the Museum.
23. **Ice House** – Built in the 19th century by Bushrod Washington. George Washington's ice house was located just below the east lawn nearer the river.
24. **Greenhouse and Slave Quarters** – Destroyed by fire in 1835 and reconstructed on the basis of documentary and archeological evidence on its original foundation. The *Museum Shop* and archeological museum are also located in the building.
25. **Upper Garden** – The boxwood

hedges are believed to have been planted in 1798 to edge the beds in which fruits and vegetables mingle with flowers in the typical eighteenth century fashion.

26. Schoolhouse or Garden House – Though identified by Washington as the "schoolhouse," there is no other reference to its use as a schoolroom.

27. Ann Pamela Cunningham Building – Administrative offices and Library. (By appointment only.)

☆ Museum Shop is located in building # 24, near entrance to the Upper Garden.

☆ Mount Vernon Inn and Gift Shop – located just outside entrance gate offers restaurant, snack bar and salesroom.

☆ Public Restrooms are located beneath the Museum, # 22.

☆ Handicapped Restrooms – available at the Mount Vernon Inn.

SMOKING PROHIBITED ON ENTIRE ESTATE

Early History of Mount Vernon

The Washington title to Mount Vernon dates from the original land grant of 1674 to John Washington, founder of the family in America and the great grandfather of George Washington. The land, then known as Little Hunting Creck Plantation, descended through the family. Augustine Washington acquired the property in 1726. Six years later in 1732, his son, George Washington, was born at Pope's Creek Plantation, another family estate in Westmoreland County, Virginia. When George was three years ald. Augustine Washington moved his family to Little Hunting Creek Plantation, where they remained for about five years.

In 1740, Augustine Washington deeded Little Hunting Creek Plantation to his son, Lawrence, George's elder half-brother. In 1743, Lawrence Washington married and settled on his plantation, renaming it Mount Vernon in honor of Admiral Edward Vernon under whom he had served in the British Navy. Augustine Washington died the same year and young George spent part of his youth at Mount Vernon with his older brother. Lawrence Washington died in 1752 and two years later George leased Mount Vernon from his brother's widow. In 1761, the title to the estate legally passed to George Washington by the terms of Lawrence Washington's will.

George Washington and Mount Vernon

In January 1759, Washington married Martha Dandridge Custis, a widow with two young children and settled at Mount Vernon with his new family. Under his skillful management, Mount Vernon became one of the outstanding estates in Virginia. He explanded the original 2,126 acres into five independently managed farms comprising nearly 8,000 acres. Early in his agricultural career, he diversified the crops raised at Mount Vernon, turning from soildepleting tobacco to wheat and other grains. The grain was ground at his mill for export as well as for use on the plantation. The Potomac River accommodated shipping and an extensive fishing industry. Mount Vernon was a largely self-sufficient community. A work force of slaves provided a wide range of skills necessary to assure that the estate ran smoothly. In a census taken the summer before his death, Washington listed 314 black men, women and children who lived and worked on the five Mount Vernon farms. Throughout his life, Washington's writings show a growing concern with the institution of slavery and the freeing of his slaves was an important provision of his will.

The development of Mount Vernon was carried out by Washington over a period of more than thirty years. He enlarged and embellished the simple farmhouse built by his father, extended the gardens and erected the outbuildings along the service lanes. With the exception of the reconstructed Coach House and Greenhouse-Slave Quarters, all these buildings have survived from Washington's time. The formal landscaping and gardens have been restored and several of the trees Washington planted along the Bowling Green still stand. The original Vaughan Plan, which may be seen in the Museum, provides a unique view of the Mansion House complex as it appeared in 1787.

The Washingtons' peaceful life at Mount Vernon was not without interruptions. At the Second Continental Congress in June, 1775, George Washington was unanimously elected commander-in-chief of the Continental Army. He visited Mount Vernon only twice during the eight years of the Revolution, on his way to and from the final victory at Yorktown in 1781. It was not until Christmas Eve of 1783 that he was at last able to return home, following the resignation of his commission to Congress.

General Washinton's retirement from public life did not last long. In the summer of 1787, he travelled to Philadelphia to preside over the Constitutional Convention. In 1789, George Washington became the first President of the United States. Except for brief visits home, he spent the next eight years in New York and Philadelphia. After concluding his second term in 1797, Washington returned to Mount Vernon where he actively managed the estate until his death on December 14, 1799. According to his wishes, he was buried in the family vault. Martha Washington died in May of 1802 and was entombed beside her husband.

Slave Burial Ground and Slavery at Mount Vernon

About fifty yards southwest of George Washington's tomb is the site of an old Mount Vernon slave burial ground. Although the area is known to have been a cemetery for slaves and free blacks who worked for the Washington family, their identities and numbes are unknown. In 1831, a visitor to Washington's tomb was told that "In front of the grave place, yonder, lie buried a hundred people of color." The only person known to have been buried there is William Lee, General Washington's personal servant during the Revolutionary War. Lee died in 1828, having been freed by Washington's will in 1799. It is believed that West Ford (1784–1863), a prominent free black, is also buried here. Ford worked as a manager for the Washington family at Mount Vernon after the General's death and later was consulted on the restoration of the estate. If any of the graves in the burial ground were originally marked, by the time the Mount Vernon Ladies' Association acquired the estate in 1858, the markers had disappeared.

When Washington began farming at Mount Vernon in 1759, the 2100 acre estate probably had a work force of about fifty slaves. The earliest surviving list of Mount Vernon slaves was drawn up by the General in 1786, after the estate had reached its fullest extent of 8000 acres. This census lists 216 men, woman and children. One hundred five of them belonged to George Washington, while the other 111 were part of the estate Martha Washington had inherited from her first husband. In July of 1799, the summer before he died, Washington drafted a final census in preparation for giving his slaves their freedom under the terms of his will. By that year, the slave population had grown to 317. This account is particularly revealing in that Washington included individual ages, occupations and family relationships. Of the 317, 124 belonged to George Washington, 153 to Martha Washington, while the remaining 40 were leased from another owner. One hundred and thirty-two of the number were either too young or too old to work.

The Mount Vernon community was largely selfsufficient and a wide range of skills were necessary to assure that it ran smoothly. Most of these skills were provided by the labor of the slaves, who carried out almost all of the essential plantation activities. Most of the slaves lived and worked on the outlying farms, where they were engaged in a variety of agricultural tasks. About one third of the working slaves were skilled in trades and crafts. They included blacksmiths, carpenters, gardeners, shoemakers, painters, brickmakers, herdsmen and coachmen. The women at the Mansion House Farm worked as spinners, weavers and seamstresses as well as cooks, dairy maids and house servants. There were also millers, coopers and distillers, who lived and worked at the mill, about a mile and a half from the Mansion, and boatmen, who operated Washington's fishing industry and his river ferry. Some of the slaves were responsible for day to day operations on the outlying farms.

While little is known about the personal lives of the Mount Vernon slaves, it is clear that marriage and family life was an important source of emotional support and stability for the slave community. Washington recognized these marriages and kept careful records of the slave families. Some were married to slaves belonging to other owners and one woman was married to a free black, indicating that the people at Mount Vernon could travel and visit other plantations. Food and clothing were distributed seasonally and Washington's personal physician was retained on a yearly basis to provide medical treatment for the slaves.

Many of the 90 slaves at the Mansion House Farm lived in the Greenhouse Quarters complex which, like the Spinning House Quarters, has been restored for exhibition.

(See numbers 22 and 18 on the Mount Vernon brochure). The living accommodations for the slaves on the outlying farms have not survived. To supplement their rations, the slaves were allowed to keep gardens and raise livestock for their households and families.

As a colonial Virginian, George Washington had been born into a world in which slavery was a part of the accepted order of things, but his attitudes underwent a gradual evolution. Changing agricultural practices had made slavery increasingly unproductive. The impact of the Revolution and Washington's concern for the future of the new American nation also influenced his thinking. After the Revolution, he had resolved never again to buy or sell a slave; *I am principaled against this kind of traffic in the human species,* he wrote, *and to disperse the families I have an aversion.* Although the system continued to have a strong hold on plantation economy, by the end of his life Washington had become convinced that emancipation was the only solution: *I wish from my soul that the Legislature of this State could see the policy of a gradual Abolition of Slavery.*

In his will, Washington provided for the freedom of his slaves after his death and left detailed instructions for the care and support of the newly friend people.

Mount Vernon is owned and maintained by the Mount Vernon Ladies' Association, a non-profit institution chartered by the Commonwealth of Virginia. Since its founding in 1853, the sole purpose of the Association has been to purchase, preserve and restore the home of George Washington for the public benefit. A modest admission fee is the principal source of income for the important ongoing work of the Association. Tax deductible contributions from the public are welcome in order to accomplish future goals without placing the entire burden on the visiting public.

The Mount Vernon Ladies' Association of the Union
MOUNT VERNON, VIRGINIA 22121
(703) 780-2000

from **The Declaration of Independence (1776)**

. . .

We hold these truths to be self-evident, that all men are created equal, that they are endowed by their Creator with certain unalienable Rights, that among these are Life, Liberty and the pursuit of Happiness.

That to secure these rights, Governments are instituted among Men, deriving their just powers from the consent of the governed, That whenever any Form of Government becomes destructive of these ends, it is the Right of the People to alter or to abolish it, and to institute a new Government, laying its foundation on such principles, and organizing its powers in such form, as to them shall seem most likely to effect their Safety and Happiness. Prudence, indeed, will dictate that Governments long established should not be changed for ligth and transient causes; and accordingly all experience hath shown, that mankind are more disposed to suffer, while evils are sufferable, than to right themselves by abolishing the forms to which they are accustomed. But when a long train of abuses and usurpations, pursuing invariably the same Object evinces a design to reduce them under absolute Despotism, it is their right, it is their duty, to throw off such Government, and to provide new Guards for their future security.

from **The Constitution of the United States (1789)**

AMENDMENT 13. (1865)
Section 1. Neither slavery nor involuntary servitude, except as a punishment for crime whereof the party shall have been duly convicted, shall exist within the United States, or any place subject to their jurisdiction.
Section 2. Congress shall have power to enforce this article by appropriate legislation.

AMENDMENT 14. (1868)
Section 1. All persons born or naturalized in the United States, and subject to the jurisdiction thereof, are citizens of the United States and of the state wherein they reside. No state shall make or enforce any law which shall abridge the privileges or immunities of citizens of the United States; nor shall any state deprive any person of life, liberty, or property without due process of law; nor deny to any person within its jurisdiction the equal protection of the law.

AMENDMENT 15. (1870)
Section 1. The right of citizens of the United States to vote shall not be denied or abridged by the United States or by any state, on account of race, color, or previous condition of servitude.
Section 2. The Congress shall have power to enforce this article by appropriate legislation.

AMENDMENT 24. (1964)
Section 1. The right of citizens of the United States to vote in any primary or other election for President or Vice-President, for electors for President or Vice-President, or for Senator or Representative in Congress, shall not be denied or abridged by the United States or any State by reason of failure to pay any poll tax or other tax.
Section 2. The Congress shall have power to enforce this article by appropriate legislation.

America's outdated constitution

The time has come for Americans to take a hard look at their Constitution. Is it up to present and future needs? The answer, clearly, is a resounding no.

Almost 200 years after its drafting, serious shortcomings are evident in the world's oldest fundamental law. Most obvious is how presidents are elected. Last year's electoral campaign was both an exercise in systematic boredom and a latter-day Roman circus.

Another shortcoming is the separation of powers – which are not separated. The Constitution established a system of separate institutions sharing powers – an invitation for a battle rather than a way to govern efficiently. No president is able to govern as does, for example, Britain's prime minister. He must negotiate treaties with Congress and interest groups. Coherent policy is impossible.

Then there is the defect of federalism, as it has evolved. The United States is split politically into 50 states, but economically it is one huge common market. That makes no constitutional sense.

The Constitution is largely an instrument to resolve domestic affairs. Those who drafted it did not foresee a technologically shrinking planet and several terrible vulnerabilities, none of which has been adequately confronted: nuclear war, population growth, the gap between rich and poor, persistent unemployment, racism, sexism, religious prejudice and the extinction of species.

The U.S. Constitution, in sum, is not up to the needs of the day. Changes should be made soon, and by design rather than, as in the past, by drift. All this suggests the need for a new constitutional convention.

Some fear another convention, believing it would be divisive. They think the Bill of Rights might be abolished, and Supreme Court decisions on such matters as school prayer and abortion reversed.

That is a counsel of despair. There will be constitutional change, and it is better to plan it than merely to react to what Alexander Hamilton called "accident and force". If France could write a new constitution, as it did in 1958, why not the United States? The United States has survived and prospered not because of the Constitution but in spite of it.

The world is far different now from that of 1787 when the Constitution was written – so different that a new structure of government should get serious attention. Thought should be given to such matters as these:

- ☆ Finding another way of electing the president.
- ☆ Moving toward a version of the parliamentary system.
- ☆ Splitting the presidency. America is the only major nation that has the same person as chief of state and head of government.
- ☆ Creating 10 to 12 regions out of the present 50 States.
- ☆ Making Congress a unicameral body of not more than 100 members.

☆ "Constitutionalizing" the giant corporations, which now, as "private" governments, rule as much as or more than public government.

All this would be no panacea, but it would help. It is time to get on with it.

From: *The US Supreme Court,* Materialien zur Lehrerfortbildung, ed. by Jürgen P. Eichler et al., Landesinstitut für Erziehung und Unterricht, Stuttgart, Nov. 1985, p. 45.

Separation of Powers and Checks and Balances

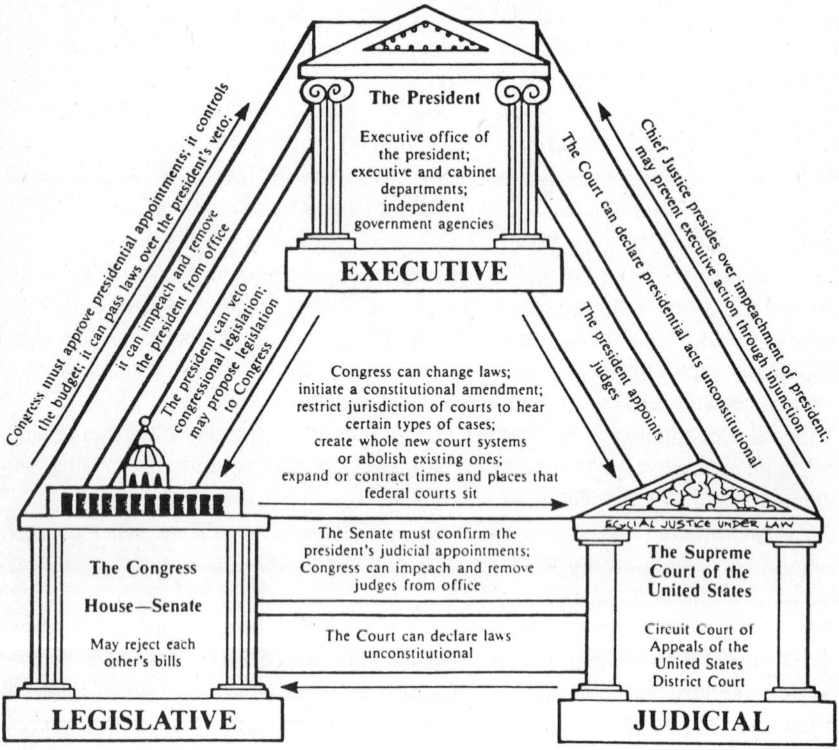

In Brief

Checks and balances

I. *Some checks on Congress and the Supreme Court made by the President*
   A. May veto bills of Congress
   B. May call special sessions of Congress
   C. May adjourn Congress if the House and Senate cannot agree on an adjournment date
   D. May withhold information from Congress
   E. Appoints Supreme Court justices

II. *Some checks on the President and the Supreme Court made by Congress*
   A. May propose amendments to the Constitution that affect offices of President and Supreme Court
   B. May impeach and try President or Supreme Court justices
   C. May override the President's veto by two-thirds vote of each house
   D. Controls all spending of money in the United States government
   E. Senate may refuse to give its consent to an appointment to the Supreme Court
   F. Senate may refuse to give its consent to any other appointments or treaties made by the President

III. *Some checks on the President and Congress made by the Supreme Court*
   A. May declare laws, passed by Congress and signed by the President, unconstitutional
   B. May bring suits or issue court orders against public officers

The executive department

I. The President and Vice-President
   A. Represent all the people of the United States
   B. Serve four-year terms
   C. Salaries
      1. President – $ 200,000 a year (in 1983)
      2. Vice-President – $ 79,125 a year
   D. Qualifications
      1. Must be at least thirty-five years old
      2. Must be a natural-born citizen
      3. Must have lived in the United States at least fourteen years
   E. Elected by electors, who are elected by the people in each state

II. The Cabinet
   A. Members in order of the establishment of their departments
      1. Secretary of State (1789)
      2. Secretary of the Treasury (1789)
      3. Secretary of Defense (originally War, 1789)
      4. Attorney General (1789)
      5. Secretary of the Interior (1849)
      6. Secretary of Agriculture (1889)
      7. Secretary of Commerce (1903)
      8. Secretary of Labor (1913)
      9. Secretary of Health and Human Services (1953, 1980)
      10. Secretary of Housing and Urban Development (1966)
      11. Secretary of Transportation (1967)
      12. Secretary of Energy (1977)
      13. Secretary of Education (1980)
   B. Serve no definite period
   C. Salary – $ 69,630 a year
   D. Appointed by the President with the consent of the Senate

The two Houses of Congress

I. The House of Representatives
   A. Representation by population – 435 members
   B. Members serve two-years terms
   C. Chairman is Speaker of the House
   D. Members' salaries
      1. Speaker – $ 79,125 a year
      2. Other members – $ 60,662.50 a year
   E. Qualifications for a member
      1. Must be at least twenty-five years old
      2. Must have been a United States citizen for seven years
      3. Must live in state he represents
   F. Members elected by the people in districts of the states they represent

II. The Senate
   A. Equal representation – two members from each state; one hundred in all
   B. Members serve six-years terms
   C. Chairmen are the Vice-President of the United States, who is President of the Senate, and the president pro tempore
   D. Members' salaries – $ 60,662.50 a year
   E. Qualifications for a member
      1. Must be at least thirty years old
      2. Must have been a United States citizen for nine years
      3. Must live in state he represents
   F. Members elected by people of states they represent

How a bill becomes a law

1. Usually prepared and introduced by a House committee, but may be introduced by any member
2. Goes to floor of House (may be sent back to committee, for further study and changes, or may not pass)
3. Wins a majority vote in House
4. Goes to Senate (usually sent to a Senate committee to be studied and perhaps amended; if amended, must be returned to House to be passed in new form – in fact, may be sent back and forth until both houses agree on wording of bill; or a compromise may be worked out by a joint committee)
5. Goes to floor of Senate (may be sent back to committee, or may not pass)
6. Wins majority vote in Senate
7. Speaker of House signs
8. President of Senate signs
9. Goes to President (may veto and send back to House with objections – House and Senate may override with two-thirds vote of each house, or may sustain veto; President may neither sign nor veto bill, in which case, becomes law in ten days without his signature; or if Congress adjourns during this time, bill receives pocket veto)
10. President signs
11. Bill becomes law

The federal judiciary

I. Regular Courts
   A. *Supreme Court*
      1. Set up by the United States Constitution
      2. Has nine justices
         a. Chief Justice
         b. Eight associate justices
      3. Has both original and appellate jurisdiction
      4. Justices serve life terms
      5. Salaries
         a. Chief Justice – $ 96,800 a year
         b. Associate justices – $ 93,000 a year
   B. *Courts of appeals*
      1. Set up by Congress for purpose of relieving the Supreme Court of having to hear all appeals from the lower federal courts
      2. Have 84 judges – eleven courts
      3. Judges serve life terms
      4. Salaries – $ 74,300 a year
      5. Have appellate jurisdiction
   C. *District courts*
      1. Set up by Congress as trial courts
      2. Have 316 judges – eighty-eight courts
      3. Judges serve life terms
      4. Salaries – $ 70,300 a year
      5. Have original jurisdiction

II. Special courts
   A. *Court of Claims*
      1. Set up by Congress to decide if certain kinds of claims (demands) against the United States or branches of its government are true and if payment of these claims should be made
      2. Has five judges
      3. Judges serve life terms
      4. Salaries – $ 74,300 a year
      5. Has original jurisdiction; appellate jurisdiction over Indian Claims Commission
      6. Located in Washington, D. C.
   B. *Court of Customs and Patent Appeals*
      1. Set up by Congress to review decisions of the Customs Court and decisions of the United States Patent Office
      2. Has five judges
      3. Judges serve life terms
      4. Salaries – $ 74,300 a year
      5. Has appellate jurisdiction
      6. Located in Washington, D. C.

C. *Court of International Trade*
   1. Set up by Congress to have jurisdiction over civil actions arising under tariff laws
   2. Has nine judges
   3. Judges serve life term
   4. Salaries – $ 70,300 a year
   5. Has original jurisdiction in controversies over value of merchandise, duties chargeable, and status of imports
   6. Located in New York, New York

D. *Tax Court*
   1. Set up by Congress to have jurisdiction over cases involving over- or underpayment of taxes
   2. Has 16 judges
   3. Judges serve life terms
   4. Salaries – $ 70,300 a year
   5. Has original jurisdiction over cases involving income, gift, estate, and personal holding company surtaxes as determined by the IRS
   6. Located in Washington, D. C.

From: *The Constitution of the United States, an Introduction,* Floyd G. Cullop, New American Library 1984

The Supreme Court

The Constitution of the United States is the basic instrument of American government and "the supreme law of the land." A state law cannot conflict with the Constitution, with national law, or with an existing treaty. The power of "judicial review" of the courts involves the right to declare acts of the legislative and executive branches of government unconstitutional. This power is based on the assumption that the Constitution is the supreme law, that acts contrary to it are void, and that the judiciary is the guardian of the Constitution. Several hundred state laws and about 100 federal laws have been declared unconstitutional by the Supreme Court. Federal courts, including the U.S. Supreme Court, act as final arbiter over questions involving the power of governmental officials at both the state and national levels. One of the most important tasks of the Supreme Court is to settle conflicts that arise between the states and the national government.

Federal courts have become involved in some of the most bitter battles in federalism. The movement to integrate schools, for example, is one in which federal-state tensions have been at their highest. The U.S. Supreme Court, however, has affirmed and reaffirmed the principle that state-run schools must be racially integrated. Applying and interpreting provisions of the federal constitution, the Supreme Court has invalidated state laws designed to block racial integration. Inferior federal courts have been even stronger. They have ordered school children to be transported ("bused") from one section of a city to another to achieve racially-balanced schools. They have ordered stubborn local school officials to go to jail or pay fines for failing to obey court orders that called for integration. They have prevented state and local governments from receiving federal money available for education; and on occasion, they have taken over the management of a school system where local officials have proven unwilling or unable to provide the court

with a satisfactory plan for racial integration. All of these actions have been taken with the understanding that federal courts, interpreting the federal constitution, have determined that no state may engage in the practice of racial segregation in matters of public education.

The Tenth Amendment provides that any powers that are not in the exclusive powers of the federal government belong to the states or to the people, respectively. For example, because the Constitution gives the federal government the exclusive power to raise an army, it would be unthinkable for individual states to start drafting men and women to form state armies; yet because the Constitution says nothing about police protection individual states may choose how to maintain and operate police forces.

Most decisions made by government reflect this compromise between federal and state power; the problem is knowing where federal power ends and state power begins, and what duplication or overlap of powers, if any, is permitted. While the authors of the Constitution attempted to enumerate all the powers delegated to the federal government, the development of the nation from a 13-state, agricultural republic in 1790 to an industrialized world power of 220 million people in 1980 has inevitably posed certain problems with respect to the demarcation of the federal – state line. The attempt to define that line, ultimately the responsibility of the *U.S. Supreme Court*, is what has produced 200 years of tension between the states and the federal government.

From: *American Studies Newsletter,* September 1985, pp. 13/14.

Issues Supreme Court Must Rule on Now

As they begin their new term, even the nation's highest-ranking judges are feeling the heat from an administration at odds with "judicial activism."

A divided, aging Supreme Court is poised to tackle some of the nation's most controversial social issues.

Affirmative action, abortion, religion and the rights of criminal suspects will all figure prominently in the new term getting under way on October 7.

The Reagan administration, which is trying to influence the Court's direction, threw down the gauntlet well before the 1985–86 term began. Atty. Gen. Edwin Meese called for a reversal of the Court's legalization of abortion and criticized barriers that, he says, the Justices have erected between church and state.

Such direct attacks, rare for an Attorney General, show how anxious conservatives are to speed change on a Court that has edged only slightly to the right in recent years. Even if the White House fails to sway the High Court this session, Prof. A. E. Dick Howard of the University of Virginia Law School says that "by hammering away now, the administration is trying to set the stage for change in the future."

Among the major issues to be reviewed this term:

Abortion. The Court's 1973 ruling legalizing abortions, *Roe v. Wade,* has long been Exhibit A for critics of "activist" rulings that create new "rights." In recent years, Justices have approved some state limits on abortion but have refused to budge from the view that women may obtain abortions under a constitutional right to privacy.

Now, the Justice Department wants the High Court to overturn *Roe v. Wade,* returning to the practice of having states adopt their own abortion policies. The 1973 abortion decision, said the department, "is so far flawed" that the Court should "abandon it." Since the initial 7-to-2 decision, abortion foes have picked up one vote: Sandra Day O'Connor, Reagan's only appointee to the Court. Analysts doubt that two others will shift their votes in cases pending this term.

Religion. A few years back, the Justices supported state tuition tax deductions for parents of parochial-school students, as well as Nativity scenes sponsored by cities. But last session, the Court struck down an Alabama law authorizing silent moments for prayer in public schools and refused to allow public teachers to work part time in parochial schools. Upset with the shift, Meese said the Court's theory that the Constitution "demands a strict neutrality between religion and irreligion would have struck the founding generation as bizarre."

At issue in one case this term is the right of public-school students to hold prayer meetings during the school day. Also being contested is Washington State's denial of vocational-rehabilitation aid to a blind man merely because he is studying for a religious career.

Handicapped infants. To prevent "medical neglect" of deformed babies – an issue that arose in the case of an Indiana newborn known as "Baby Doe" – the Reagan administration issued rules threatening to end aid to hospitals that withhold nourishment from such infants. Hospital officials sued, charging that the issue isn't covered by federal law. Justices agreed to decide the issue, which is being watched closely by "right to life" groups, parents and doctors.

Racial discrimination. Last year, the Court ruled against black Memphis firefighters, hired under an affirmative-action plan, who argued that they should have been protected from layoffs. The administration argues that the ruling bars all quotas in employment-bias cases, but many lower courts have rejected that notion.

Now, the Justices will weigh in again. In a dispute over a quota in a union contract, white Michigan teachers complain that they lost their jobs while minorities were retained. The Justice Department sides with the whites, noting that government should not "advance some and suppress others . . . because of the color of their skin."

Criminal law. Defendants are making new pleas to increase legal protections. In one case, a Mississippi man contends that he should not have been sentenced to death as an accomplice in a murder because he did not intend to commit the crime. Three other appeals ask the High Court to set standards for measuring racial prejudice in jury selection – a recurring issue because a disproportionate number of defendants are from minority groups.

The Justices are bound to change legal doctrine on some issues, but abrupt shifts across the board are unlikely, given the remarkable stability of the Court's personnel. Although five Justices are over 75 jears old, senior advisers insist that Reagan has designated no favored candidate should a vacancy arise. But among those sure to be considered: Judges Robert Bork and Antonin Scalia of the U.S.

appeals court in Washington, D.C., U.S. Appeals Judge Anthony Kennedy of Sacramento and William Clark, a former top aide to the President.

An opening at the High Court would bolster conservative forces, who include Chief Justice Warren Burger, William Rehnquist and O'Connor, and would add to the excitement of a term that already promises to be a tumultuous one.«

From: U.S. NEWS & WORLD REPORT, Oct. 14, 1985

Federal Powers – State Powers

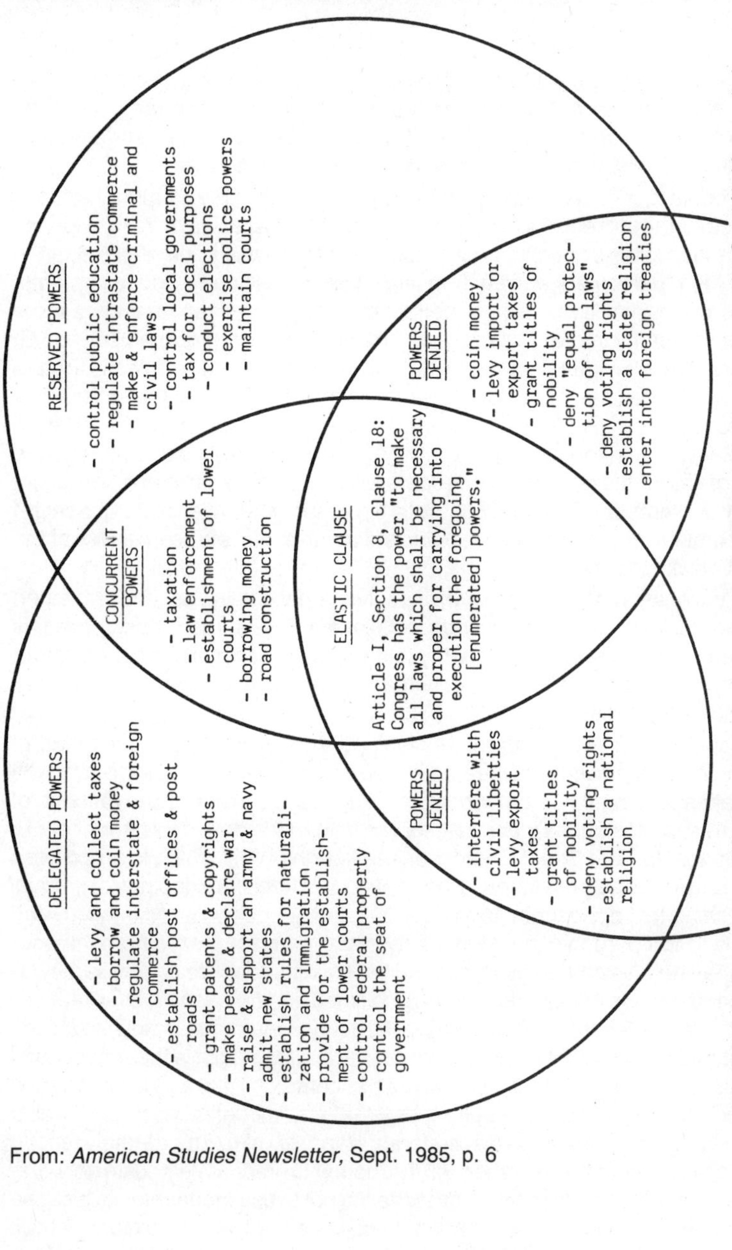

DELEGATED POWERS: also called **enumerated** powers, are powers specifically listed in the Constitution as being granted to the federal government (Constitution, Article I, Section 8, Clauses 1-18).

RESERVED POWERS: also called **residual** powers, are powers not given to the federal government but reserved to the states or the people (Constitution, 10th Amendment).

CONCURRENT POWERS: powers which may be exercised by both the federal government and state governments.

ELASTIC CLAUSE: enables Congress to expand its (enumerated/delegated) powers and to assume "implied" powers.

From: *American Studies Newsletter*, Sept. 1985, p. 6

The First Issue of *The Liberator, 1831*

In the month of August, I issued proposals for publishing *The Liberator* in Washington city; but the enterprise, though hailed in different sections of the country, was palsied by public indifference. Since that time, the removal of the *Genius of Universal Emancipation* to the Seat of Government has rendered less imperious the establishment of a similar periodical in that quarter.

During my recent tour for the purpose of exciting the minds of the people by a series of discourses on the subject of slavery, every place that I visited gave fresh evidence of the fact, that a greater revolution in public sentiment was to be effected in the free states – *and particularly in New England* – than at the south. I found contempt more bitter, opposition more active, detraction more relentless, prejudice more stubborn, and apathy more frozen, than among slave owners themselves. Of course, there were individual exceptions to the contrary. This state of things afflicted, but did not dishearten me. I determined, at every hazard, to lift up the standard of emancipation in the eyes of the nation, *within sight of Bunker Hill and in the birth place of liberty.* That standard is now unfurled; and long may it float, unhurt by the spoliations of time or the missiles of a desperate foe – yea, till every chain be broken, and every bondman set free! Let Southern oppressors tremble – let their secret abettors tremble – let their Northern apologists tremble – let all the enemies of the persecuted blacks tremble.

I deem the publication of my original Prospectus unnecessary, as it has obtained a wide circulation. The principles therein inculcated will be steadily pursued in this paper, excepting that I shall not array myself as the political partisan of any man. In defending the great cause of human rights, I wish to derive the assistance of all religions and of all parties.

Assenting to the "self evident truth" maintained in the American Declaration of Independence, "that all men are created equal, and endowed by their Creator with certain unalienable rights – among which are life, liberty and the pursuit of happiness," I shall strenuously contend for the immediate enfranchisement of our slave population. In Park Street Church, on the Fourth of July, 1829, in an address on slavery, I unreflectingly assented to the popular but pernicious doctrine of *gradual* abolition. I seize this opportunity to make a full and unequivocal recantation, and thus publicly to ask pardon of my God, of my country, and of my brethren the poor slaves, for having uttered a sentiment so full of timidity, injustice and absurdity. A similar recantation, from my pen, was published in the *Genius of Universal Emancipation* at Baltimore, in September, 1829. My conscience is now satisfied.

I am aware, that many object to the severity of my language; but is there not cause for severity? I *will* be as harsh as truth, and as uncompromising as justice. On this subject, I do not wish to think, or speak, or write, with moderation. No! no! Tell a man whose house is on fire, to give a moderate alarm; tell him to moderately rescue his wife from the hands of the ravisher; tell the mother to gradually extricate her babe from the fire into which it has fallen; – but urge me not to use moderation in a cause like the present. I am in earnest – I will not equivocate – I will not excuse – I will not retreat a single inch – AND I WILL BE HEARD. The apathy of the people is enough to make every statue leap from its pedestal, and to hasten the resurrection of the dead.

It is pretended, that I am retarding the cause of emancipation by the coarseness of my invective and the precipitancy of my measures. *The charge is not true.* On this question my influence, – humble as it is, – is felt at this moment to a considerable extent, and shall be felt in coming years – not perniciously, but beneficially – not as a curse, but as a blessing; and posterity will bear testimony that I was right. I desire to thank God, that he enables me to disregard "the fear of man which bringeth a snare," and to speak his truth in its simplicity and power.

And here I close with this fresh dedication:

"Oppression! I have seen thee, face to face,
And met thy cruel eye and cloudy brow;
But thy soul-withering glance I fear not now –
For dread to prouder feelings doth give place
Of deep abhorrence! Scorning the disgrace
Of slavish knees that at thy footstool bow,
I also kneel – but with far other bow
Do hail thee and thy herd of hirelings base: –
I swear, while life-blood warms my throbbing veins,
Still to oppose and thwart, with heart and hand,
Thy brutalizing sway – till Afric's chains
Are burst, and Freedom rules the rescued land, –
Trampling Oppression and his iron rod:
Such is the vow I take – SO HELP ME GOD!"

William Lloyd Garrison, "Preface to The First Issue of The Liberator, 1831", in Richard D. Heffner, *A Documentary History of the United States,* New American Library, 1976.

The Dred Scott Decision (1857)

Dred Scott (c. 1795–1858) lived most of his life as an obscure, illiterate slave. In the 1830s, Scott had been purchased by Army surgeon John Emerson and accompanied his master to military posts in the free state of Illinois and Wisconsin Territory, where slavery was barred under the *Missouri Compromise* of 1820. After Emerson's death in 1844, his widow inherited Scott. Mrs Emerson opposed slavery, but instead of giving Scott his freedom, she agreed to allow several antislavery men, including the son of Scott's original owner, to seek a court decision on the rights of a slave who had lived in free territory. Scott's lawyers sued Mrs Emerson, and a lower court in St. Louis declared Scott free, but the Missouri Supreme Court in 1852 returned him to servitude. At this time Mrs Emerson married Dr. C. C. Chaffee, an abolitionist congressman from Massachusetts, who decided to use Scott to launch another legal attack on slavery. As an abolitionist congressman, Dr. Chaffee did not want to be sued by Scott's lawyers, for the action would have seemed too obviously contrived as a test case. So he "sold" Scott to his wife's brother, J. F.

Sandford of New York, and the case of *Dred Scott v. Sandford* reached the U.S. Supreme Court in 1856.

In March 1857, Chief Justice Roger B. Taney announced the decision of the court. By a seven to two vote it denied Scott his freedom on the grounds that he remained a slave in Missouri and therefore had no right to sue. In his written opinion, the Chief Justice stated that blacks had since the time of the Declaration of Independence been regarded "as beings of an inferior order . . . who had no rights a white man was bound to respect," and no Negro could be a citizen of any state regardless of whether he was a slave or free. Therefore, no Negro was ever entitled to sue. If Taney had ended his opinion there, the outcry against the court might not have been so widerspread and bitter throughout the North. But he went on to say that even were Scott accorded the right to sue, he would lose his case, since the mere fact of his having lived in free territory did not make him a free man. This was so, said Taney, because the Fifth Amendment to the U.S. Constitution provides that no person be deprived of his property without due process of law; therefore, the Missouri Compromise, which prohibited slavery in the Wisconsin Territory, was unconstitutional – because it denied a slave owner the right to take his property into that territory without running the risk of loss.

Throughout the North, defiance of the court's "wicked and false" judgment was proclaimed while supporters of slavery in the South rejoiced.

As for Scott, his owner freed him a few days after the court decision, and he worked at odd jobs in St. Louis until his death in 1858.

From: *The US Supreme Court,* Materialien zur Lehrerfortbildung, ed. by Jürgen P. Eichler et al., Landesinstitut für Erziehung und Unterricht, Stuttgart, Nov. 1985, p. 39.

The Emancipation Proclamation, *1863*

Whereas on the twenty-second day of September, in the year of our Lord one thousand eight hundred and sixty-two, a proclamation was issued by the President of the United States, containing, among other things, the following, to wit:

That on the first day of January, in the year of our Lord one thousand eight hundred and sixty-three, all persons held as slaves within any State, or designated part of a State, the people whereof shall then be in rebellion against the United States, shall be then, thenceforward, and forever free; and the Executive Government of the United States, including the military and naval authority thereof, will recognize and maintain the freedom of such persons, and will do no act or acts to repress such persons, or any of them, in any efforts they may make for their actual freedom . . .

Now, therefore, I, Abraham Lincoln, President of the United States, by virtue of the power in me vested as Commander-in-Chief of the Army and Navy of the United States, in time of actual armed rebellion against the authority and government of the United States, and as a fit and necessary war measure for suppressing said rebellion, do, on this first day of January, in the year of our Lord one thousand eight hundred and sixty-three, . . . order and designate as the States and parts of States wherein the people thereof, respectively, are this day in rebellion against the United States, the following, to wit:

Arkansas, Texas, Louisiana (except the parishes of St. Bernard, Plaquemines, Jefferson, St. John, St. Charles, St. James, Ascension, Assumption, Terre Bonne, Lafourche, St. Mary, St. Martin, and Orleans, including the city of New Orleans), Mississippi, Alabama, Florida, Georgia, South Carolina, North Carolina, and Virginia (except the forty-eight counties designated as West Virginia, and also the counties of Berkeley, Accomac, Northampton, Elizabeth City, York, Princess Anne, and Norfolk, including the cities of Norfolk and Portsmouth), and which excepted parts are for the present left precisely as if this proclamation were not issued.

And by virtue of the power and for the purpose aforesaid, I do order and declare that all persons held as slaves within said designated States and parts of States are, and henceforward shall be, free; and that the Executive Government of the United States, including the military and naval authorities thereof, shall recognize and maintain the freedom of said persons.

And I hereby enjoin upon the people so declared to be free to abstain from all violence, unless in necessary selfdefense; and I recommend to them that, in all cases where allowed, they labor faithfully for reasonable wages.

And I further declare and make known that such persons of suitable condition will be received into the armed service of the United States to garrison forts, positions, stations, and other places, and to man vessels of all sorts in said service.

And upon this act, sincerely believed to be an act of justice, warranted by the Constitution upon military necessity, I invoke the considerate judgment of mankind and the gracious favor of Almighty God.

In witness whereof, I have hereunto set my hand and caused the seal of the United States to be affixed.

Done at the city of Washington, the first day of January, in the year of our Lord one thousand eight hundred and sixty-three, and of the independence of the United States of America the eighty-seventh.

By the President: ABRAHAM LINCOLN

WILLIAM H. SEWARD, Secretary of State.

From: Richard D. Hefner, *op. cit.,* pp. 155–157.

Plessy v. Ferguson, 1896

This case wrote the **separate but equal** doctrine into American constitutional law. It was, in effect, reversed in Brown v. Topeka, Doc. no. 617. See Vann Woodward, *The Strange Career of Jim Crow;* Gilbert Stephenson, *Race Distinctions in American Law;* Rayford Logan, *Negro in American Life and Thought 1877–1901;* and refs. to Doc. 617.

BROWN, J.[1] This case turns upon the constitutionality of an act of the general

[1] Chief Justice

assembly of the state of Louisiana, passed in 1890, providing for separate railway carriages for the white and colored races. . . .

The constitutionality of this act is attacked upon the ground that it conflicts both with the 13th Amendment of the Constitution, abolishing slavery, and the 14th Amendment, which prohibits certain restrictive legislation on the part of the states.

1. That it does not conflict with the 13th Amendment, which abolished slavery and involuntary servitude, except as a punishment for crime, is too clear for argument. . . .

A statute which implies merely a legal distinction between the white and colored races – a distinction which is founded in the color of the two races, and which must always exist so long as white men are distinguished from the other race by color – has no tendency to destroy the legal equality of the two races, or re-establish a state of involuntary servitude. Indeed, we do not understand that the 13th Amendment is strenuously relied upon by the plaintiff in error in this connection. . . .

The object of the amendment was undoubtedly to enforce the absolute equality of the two races before the law, but in the nature of things it could not have been intended to abolish distinctions based upon color, or to enforce social, as distinguished from political, equality, or a commingling of the two races upon terms unsatisfactory to either. Laws permitting, and even requiring their separation in places where they are liable to be brought into contact do not necessarily imply the inferiority of either race to the other, and have been generally, if not universally, recognized as within the competency of the state legislatures in the exercise of their police power. The most common instance of this is connected with the establishment of separate schools for white and colored children, which have been held to be a valid exercise of the legislative power even by courts of states where the political rights of the colored race have been longest and most earnestly enforced. . . .

It is claimed by the plaintiff in error that, in any mixed community, the reputation of belonging to the dominant race, in this instance the white race is *property,* in the same sense that a right of action, or of inheritance, is property. Conceding this to be so, for the purposes of this case, we are unable to see how this statute deprives him of, or in any way affects his right to, such property. If he be a white man and assigned to a colored coach, he may have his action for damages against the company for being deprived of his so-called property. Upon the other hand, if he be a colored man and be so assigned, he has been deprived of no property, since he is not lawfully entitled to the reputation of being a white man. . . .

So far, then, as a conflict with the 14th Amendment is concerned, the case reduces itself to the question whether the statute of Louisiana is a reasonable regulation, and with respect to this there must necessarily be a large discretion on the part of the legislature. In determining the question of reasonableness it is at liberty to act with reference to the established usages, customs, and traditions of the people, and with a view to the promotion of their comfort, and the preservation of the public peace and good order. Gauged by this standard, we cannot say that a law which authorizes or even requires the separation of the two races in public conveyances is unreasonable or more abnoxious to the 14th Amendment than the acts of Congress requiring separate schools for colored children in the District of Columbia, the constitutionality of which does not seem to have been questioned, or the corresponding acts of state legislatures.

We consider the underlying fallacy of the plaintiff's argument to consist in the assumption that the enforced separation of the two races stamps the colored race with a badge of inferiority. If this be so, it is not by reason of anything found in the act, but solely because the colored race chooses to put that construction upon it. The argument necessarily assumes that if, as has been more than once the case, and is not unlikely to be so again, the colored race should become the dominant power in the state legislature, and should enact a law in precisely similar terms, it would thereby relegate the white race to an inferior position. We imagine that the white race, at least, would not acquiesce in this assumption. The argument also assumes that social prejudice may be overcome by legislation, and that equal rights cannot be secured to the Negro except by an enforced commingling of the two races. We cannot accept this proposition. If the two races are to meet on terms of social equality, it must be the result of natural affinities, a mutual appreciation of each other's merits and a voluntary consent of individuals. . . . Legislation is powerless to eradicate racial instincts or to abolish distinctions based upon physical differences, and the attempt to do so can only result in accentuating the difficulties of the present situation. If the civil and political right of both races be equal, one cannot be inferior (552) to the other civilly or politically. If one race be inferior to the other socially, the Constitution of the United States cannot put them upon the same plane.

From: *Documents of American History,* ed. by Henry S. Commager

Brown v. Board of Education of Topeka, 1954 (see also p. 140 ff.)

WARREN, C. J. These cases come to us from the States of Kansas, South Carolina, Virginia, and Delaware.

In each of the cases, minors of the Negro race, through their legal representatives, seek the aid of the courts in obtaining admission to the public schools of their community on a nonsegregated basis. In each instance, they have been denied admission to schools attended by white children under laws requiring or permitting segregation according to race. This segregation was alleged to deprive the plaintiffs of the equal protection of the laws under the Fourteenth Amendment. In each of the cases other than the Delaware case, a three-judge federal district court denied relief to the plaintiffs on the so-called "separate but equal" doctrine announced by this Court in *Plessy v. Ferguson.* Under that doctrine, equality of treatment is accorded when the races are provided substantially equal facilities, even though these facilities be separate. In the Delaware case, the Supreme Court of Delaware adhered to that doctrine, but ordered that the plaintiffs be admitted to the white schools because of their superiority to the Negro schools.

The plaintiffs contend that segregated public schools are not "equal" and cannot be made "equal", and that hence they are deprived of the equal protection of the laws. Because of the obvious importance of the question presented, the Court took jurisdiction.

Today, education is perhaps the most important function of state and local governments. Compulsory school attendance laws and the great expenditures for education both demonstrate our recognition of the importance of education to our democratic society. It is required in the performance of our most basic public responsibilities, even service in the armed forces. It is the very foundation of good citizenship. Today it is a principal instrument in awakening the child to cultural values, in preparing him for later professional training, and in helping him to adjust normally to his environment. In these days, it is doubtful that any child may reasonably be expected to succeed in life if he is denied the opportunity of an education. Such an opportunity, where the state has undertaken to provide it, is a right which must be made available to all on equal terms.

We come then to the question presented: Does segregation of children in public schools solely on the basis of race, even though the physical facilities and other "tangible" factors may be equal, deprive the children of the minority group of equal educational opportunities? We believe that it does.

To separate them from others of similar age and qualifications solely because of their race generates a feeling of inferiority as to their status in the community that may affect their hearts and minds in a way unlikely ever to be undone.

We conclude that in the field of public education the doctrine of "separate but equal" has no place. Separate educational facilities are inherently unequal. Therefore, we hold that the plaintiffs and others similarly situated for whom the actions have been brought are, by reason of the segregation complained of, deprived of the equal protection of the laws guaranteed by the Fourteenth Amendment.

From: DOCUMENTS OF AMERICAN HISTORY. Edited by Henry Steele Commager.

Kennedy Address on Civil Rights

Nation-wide Radio and Television Address made by President Kennedy from the White House on Tuesday, June 11th, 1963.

Good Evening, My Fellow Citizens.

This afternoon, following a series of threats and defiant statements, the presence of Alabama National Guardsmen was required on the University of Alabama to carry out the final and unequivocal order of the United States District Court of the Northern District of Alabama. That order called for the admission of two clearly qualified young Alabama residents who happened to have been born Negro.

That they were admitted peacefully on the campus is due in good measure to the conduct of the students of the University of Alabama, who met their responsibilities in a constructive way.

I hope that every American, regardless of where he lives, will stop and examine his conscience about this and other related incidents. This nation was founded by men of many nations and backgrounds. It was founded on the principle that all men are created equal, and that the rights of every man are diminished when the rights of one man are threatened.

Today we are committed to a worldwide struggle to promote and protect the rights of all who wish to be free, and when Americans are sent to Vietnam or West Berlin, we do not ask for whites only. It ought to be possible, therefore, for American students of any color to attend any public institution they select without having to be backed up by troops. It ought to be possible for American consumers of any color to receive equal service in places of public accommodation, such as hotels and restaurants and theaters and retail stores, without being forced to resort to demonstrations in the street, and it ought to be possible for American citizens of any color to register and vote in a free election without interference or fear of reprisal. But this is not the case.

The Negro baby born in America today, regardless of the section of the nation in which he is born, has about one-half as much chance of completing high school as a white baby born in the same place on the same day, one-third as much chance of completing college, one-third as much chance of becoming a professional man, twice as much chance of becoming unemployed, about one-seventh as much chance of earning $ 10,000 a year, a life expectancy which is seven years shorter, and the prospects of earning only half as much.

This is not a sectional issue. Difficulties over segregation and discrimination exist in every city, in every State of the Union, producing in many cities a rising tide of discontent that threatens the public safety. Nor is this a partisan issue in a time of domestic crisis. Men of good will and generosity should be able to unite regardless of party or politics. This is not even a legal or legislative issue alone. It is better to settle these matters in the courts than on the streets, and new laws are needed at every level, but law alone cannot make men see right. We are confronted primarily with a moral issue.

It is as old as the scriptures and is as clear as the American Constitution. The heart of the question is whether all Americans are to be afforded equal right and equal opportunities, whether we are going to treat our fellow Americans as we want to be treated. If an American, because his skin is dark, cannot eat lunch in a restaurant open to the public, if he cannot send his children to the best public school available, if he cannot vote for the public officials who represent him, if, in short, he cannot enjoy the full and free life which all of us want, then who among us would be content to have the color of his skin changed and stand in his place? Who among us would then be content with the counsels of patience and delay? 100 years of delay have passed since President Lincoln freed the slaves, yet their heirs, their grandsons, are not fully free. They are not yet freed from the bonds of injustice. They are not yet freed from social and economic oppression, and this nation, for all its hopes and all its boasts, will not be fully free until all its citizens are free.

We preach freedom around the world, and we mean it, and we cherish our freedom here at home, but are we to say to the world, and much more importantly, to each other that this is a land of the free except for the Negroes; that we have no class or caste system, no ghettoes, no master race except with respect to Negroes?

The fires of frustration and discord are burning in every city, north and south, where legal remedies are not at hand. Redress is sought in the streets, in demonstrations, parades and protests which create tensions and threaten violence and threaten lives.

We face, therefore, a moral crisis as a country and as a people. It cannot be met by repressive police action. It cannot be left to increased demonstrations in the streets. It cannot be quieted by token moves or talk. It is time to act in the Congress, in your State and local legislative body and, above all, in all of our daily lives.

Next week I shall ask the Congress of the United States to act, to make a commitment it has not fully made in this century to the proposition that race has no place in American life or law. The Federal judiciary has upheld that proposition in a series of forthright cases. The executive branch has adopted that proposition in the conduct of its affairs, including the employment of Federal personnel, the use of Federal facilities, and the sale of Federally financed housing.

But there are other necessary measures which only the Congress can provide, and they must be provided at this session. The old code of equity law under which we live demands for every wrong a remedy, but in too many communities, in too many parts of the country, wrongs are inflicted on Negro citizens as there are no remedies at law. Unless the Congress acts, their only remedy is the street.

I am, therefore, asking the Congress to enact legislation giving all Americans the right to be served in facilities which are open to the public – hotels, restaurants, theaters, retail stores, and similar establishments.

I am also asking Congress to authorize the Federal Government to participate more fully in lawsuits designed to end segregation in public education. We have succeeded in persuading many districts to desegregate voluntarily. Dozens have admitted Negroes without violence. Today a Negro is attending a State-supported institution in every one of our 50 States, but the pace is very slow. Too many Negro children entering segregated grade schools at the time of the Supreme Court's decision nine years ago will enter segregated high schools this fall, having suffered a loss which can never be restored. The lack of an adequate education denies the Negro a chance to get a decent job.

Other features will also be requested, including greater protection for the right to vote. But legislation, I repeat, cannot solve this problem alone. It must be solved in the homes of every American in every community across our country.

In this respect, I want to pay tribute to those citizens north and south who have been working in their communities to make life better for all. They are acting not out of a sense of legal duty but out of a sense of human decency.

Like our soldiers and sailors in all parts of the world, they are meeting freedom's challenge on the firing line, and I salute them for their honor and their courage.

Civil Rights Act of 1964
July 2, 1964

Dissatisfaction with the ineffectiveness of the Civil Rights Act of 1957 had led to the passage of another civil-rights law in 1960, addressed primarily to the problem of voting but, like its predecessor, ineffective. Mounting pressure from the civil-rights movement forced President Kennedy in 1963 to demand federal legislation against segregation in all businesses involved in interstate commerce and against job discrimination. President Johnson continued Kennedy's efforts. After a long struggle, capped by a three-month filibuster, Congress finally passed a bill, stronger than Kennedy's original proposal but weaker than some of the alternatives proposed by the House. It prohibited discrimination in places of public accommodation, forbade discrimination in employment, forbade discrimination in voting, and set up machinery of enforcement. This was the strongest civilrights measure since Reconstruction, but in practice it was a qualified success at best.

TITLE I – VOTING RIGHTS

Sec. 101 (2). No person acting under color of law shall –

(A) in determining whether any individual is qualified under State law or laws to vote in any Federal election, apply any standard, practice, or procedure different from the standards, practices, or procedures applied under such law or laws to other individuals within the same county, parish, or similar political subdivision who have been found by State officials to be qualified to vote; . . .

(C) employ any literacy test as a qualification for voting in any Federal election unless (i) such test is administered to each individual wholly in writing; and (ii) a certified copy of the test and of the answers given by the individual is furnished to him within twenty-five days of the submission of his request made within the period of time during which records and papers are required to be retained and preserved pursuant to title III of the Civil Rights Act of 1960. . . .

TITLE II – INJUNCTIVE RELIEF AGAINST DISCRIMINATION IN PLACES OF PUBLIC ACCOMMODATION

Sec. 201. (a) All persons shall be entitled to the full and equal enjoyment of the goods, services, facilities, privileges, advantages, and accommodations of any place of public accommodation, as defined in this section, without discrimination or segregation on the ground of race, color, religion, or national origin.

(b) Each of the following establishments which serves the public is a place of public accommodation within the meaning of this title if its operations affect commerce, or if discrimination or segregation by it is supported by State action:

(1) any inn, motel, or other establishment which provides lodging to transient guests, other than an establishment located within a building which contains not more than five rooms for rent or hire and which is actually occupied by the proprietor of such establishment as his residence;

(2) any restaurant, cafeteria, lunch room, lunch counter, soda fountain, or other facility principally engaged in selling food for consumption on the premises . . .

(3) any motion picture house, theater, concert hall, sports arena, stadium or other place of exhibition or entertainment. . . .

(d) Discrimination or segregation by an establishment is supported by State action within the meaning of this title if such discrimination or segregation (1) is carried on under color of any law, statute, ordinance, or regulation; or (2) is carried on under color of any custom or usage required or enforced by officials of the State or political subdivision thereof. . . .

Sec. 202. All persons shall be entitled to be free, at any establishment or place, from discrimination or segregation of any kind on the ground of race, color, religion, or national origin, if such discrimination or segregation is or purports to be required by any law, statute, ordinance, regulation, rule, or order of a State or any agency or political subdivision thereof. . . .

Sec. 206. (a) Whenever the Attorney General has reasonable cause to believe that any person or group of persons is engaged in a pattern or practice of resistance to the full enjoyment of any of the rights secured by this title, the Attorney General may bring a civil action in the appropriate district court of the United States by filing with it a complaint . . . requesting such preventive relief, including an application for a permanent or temporary injunction, restraining order or other order against the person or persons responsible for such pattern or practice, as he deems necessary to insure the full enjoyment of the rights herein described.

TITLE VI – NONDISCRIMINATION IN FEDERALLY ASSISTED PROGRAMS
Sec. 601. No person in the United States shall, on the ground of race, color, or national origin, be excluded from participation in, be denied the benefits of, or be subjected to discrimination under any program or activity receiving Federal financial assistance.

From: *Documents of American History,* ed. by H. S. Commager

How two cases reached the Supreme Court

While there are certain cases that can be brought directly to the Supreme Court, the majority of the cases are brought on appeal. If either party in a case is unhappy with the decision of a lower court, it has the right to appeal that decision to a higher court. An appeal is not a new trial, but rather a reexamination of the evidence, procedures and legal or constitutional principles on which the decision was based in the previous trial. Only a very small percentage of cases appealed are considered by the Supreme Court. During its 1976–77 term, the Court received petitions for 4, 731 cases, yet agreed to hear oral arguments for only 176. Generally speaking, the Court will be inclined to hear a case if it involves a basic constitutional principle, an important question of federal law or a conflict between state and federal law. Appeals are brought to the U.S. Supreme Court from the highest courts in each state or from lower federal courts. The diagrams below illustrate these two paths by which a case reaches the Supreme Court.

From State Supreme Court
GIDEON v. WAINRIGHT

ACOUSED OF A CRIME
June 1961 – Clarence Earl Gideon was arrested and charged with breaking and entering the Bay Harbor Poolroom in Panama City, Florida.

From Federal District Court
BROWN v. BOARD OF EDUCATION

"MY RIGHTS HAVE BEEN VIOLATED"
September 1950 – An eight-year-old black student named Linda Brown was denied admission to an all-white elementary school in Topeka, Kansas.

TRIAL IN STATE CIRCUIT COURT

1961 – Gideon was too poor to afford a lawyer, but his request for a court-appointed lawyer was rejected. Judge Robert L. McCrary cited Florida state law and the 1942 U.S. Supreme Court decision BETTS v. BRADY. Gideon served as his own lawyer, but lost the case. He was found guilty and given the maximum five-year sentence.

APPEAL TO THE STATE SUPREME COURT

October 1961 – The Supreme Court of the State of Florida denied Gideon's petition of appeal. It upheld the lower court's ruling that there was no legal requirement to appoint a lawyer for Gideon.

APPEAL TO THE UNITED STATES SUPREME COURT

June 1962 – The U.S. Supreme Court agreed to hear the GIDEON case in its next session.

June 1962 – The Supreme Court appointed Abe Fortas, a prominent Washington attorney, to represent Gideon. Despite its own BETTS v. BRADY decision, the Supreme Court had traditionally appointed lawyers for poor defendants.

January 1963 – Oral arguments were heard between Abe Fortas and Florida assistant attorney General Bruce Jacob.

THE SUPREME COURT DECIDES

March 1963 – The Court rules in favor of Gideon, holding that he was entitled to a court-appointed lawyer. They directed the State of Florida to give Gideon a new trial and to appoint a lawyer to

TRIAL IN FEDERAL DISTRICT COURT

February 1951 – Her father, Oliver Brown, and 12 other black parents sued the city's Board of Education in the United States District Court. The case was officially titled BROWN v. BOARD OF EDUCATION OF TOPEKA, KANSAS.

APPEAL TO THE UNITED STATES SUPREME COURT

While many cases must be appealed from district court to the court of appeals, this case was appealed directly to the Supreme Court.

June 1952 – The Supreme Court agreed to hear the BROWN case.

December 1952 – Arguments were heard from lawyers for both sides. However, the Court was divided and unable to arrive at a decision.

December 1953 – A year later, arguments were again heard for both sides. During that time, a significant change had occured on the Court. Chief Justice Fred Vinson had died in September and President Eisenhower had appointed Earl Warren to replace him.

THE SUPREME COURT DECIDES

May 1954 – By a 9 to 0 vote the Supreme Court overruled the district court's decision. It states that segregated schools were unconstitutional because segregation "deprives children of the minority represent him. The greater effect was that all persons would now be guaranteed a lawyer.

August 1963 – Gideon was represented by a court-appointed lawyer at a new trial in the Circuit Court of Florida. He was found not guilty.

From: *The US Supreme Court,* pp. 38/39

group of equal educational opportunities." It nullified the "separate but equal" principle of the 1896 PLESSY v. FERGUSON case.

Words You Need To Know (referring to pp. 120–142)

abridge	restrict; take away
absentee ballot	official mail-in-ballot
adjourn	close a meeting until some future date
advocate	call for; speak or write in favour of
affirm	promise on one's honour
ambassador	official representative of one government to another
appoint	name to take office
appeal	request for new trial in a higher court
appelate jurisdiction	power to re-try a case already tried in a lower court
apportion	divide
appraisal	estimated worth; value placed upon
appropriate	necessary; needed
appropriation	amount set aside for a special purpose
arsenal	storage place for weapons
assembly	gathering of people
attested	witnessed
authority	here: power
bail	a sum of money put up by an arrested person to insure his return, in order to be released until the time of his trial
bill	proposed law
bill of attainder	a law that punishes a single individual and denies him the right to a trial
bounty	reward
bribery	payment for favours that cause the breaking of the trust of office
Cabinet	the President's advisers, who head executive departments

candidate	person seeking election to office
caucus	meeting of leaders of a political party held for some special purpose
census	count of the people in any given place
certify	make, official; declare true
Chief Executive	President of the United States
civil case	court case concerning a disagreement between parties
civil suit	court case involving a dispute between parties
claims	demands made against
commerce	trade; business
commission	give official recognition
committee	group set up for some special purpose
compact	agreement; contract
compensation	payment for goods or services
confederation	loosely joined group of states that gives only limited powers to a central government, with each state keeping the most important powers for itself
confess	admit; tell
confirm	approve
conflict	differ; disagree
Congress	US national legislature (House of Representatives and the Senate)
Congressional district	section of a state that is represented by one member of the House
consul	official who watches over commercial interests
constitution	laws and principles according to which a state is governed
controversy	prolonged argument, esp. over social, moral or political matters
convention	meeting held for a special reason
counsel	lawyer; attorney; legal advice of a lawyer
counterfeit	imitation; false
debate	argument
decision	judgement; ruling
defendant	person against whom a legal action is brought
delegate	elected representative sent to a conference or meeting
denied	not allowed; prohibited
domestic	of the home; native; of one's own country
domestic violence	riots; mob action

double jeopardy	being tried again for a crime already not found guilty of
effects	personal property
elastic clause	power given to Congress to make laws to see that its other powers are carried out
elector	person elected by the people of a state to cast a vote for the President
electoral college	all the electors in the USA
emancipate	set free
emolument	payment for service
enumeration	number; count
equity case	case concerning asking for court action to prevent a wrong or end a wrong
evidence	information; facts
exceed	go beyond
excise	tax on the manufacture, sale, or use of goods within a country
executive	person who sees that acts are carried out
expel	remove
extradition	the return of a fugitive by one authority to another
federation	a tightly joined group of states giving certain powers, duties, and responsibilities that can be best carried out in the interest of all the states to a central government
felony	a serious crime
forfeiture	loss of property as payment for a wrong act
fugitive	one who flees; one escaping from the law
general election	any regular election to fill public offices
grand jury	twelve to twenty-three persons selected to decide if evidence against an accused person is sufficient for holding a trial
guarantee	assure
imminent	near; immediate
impartial	open-minded; not prejudiced
impeachment	act of accusing a public official of wrongdoing
impeachment trial	act of deciding innocence or guilt of impeached official
impost	tax on imports
inauguration	ceremony connected with taking office
indictment	formal accusation

indict	charge with a crime and hold for trial
ineligible	unable to meet certain qualifications for membership
inferior	lower in rank
inferior courts	courts lower than the Supreme Court
insurrection	rebellion
introduce	bring up; make known
invasion	
involuntary servitude	work done against one's will
judicial	pertaining to courts
judicial branch	the United States system of courts
judiciary	the judges of a State collectively; system of law courts in a country
jurisdiction	power to try a case
jury	group selected to decide innocence or guilt of an accused person on trial
justice	fair treatment
lay	raise; collect
legislation	laws
legislative	lawmaking
legislature	law-making body
literacy	ability to read and write
lobby	a special interest group which tries to get laws passed in its interests or keep laws that are against its interests from being passed
migration	movement from one place to another
militia	state armed force; National Guard
misdemeanors	crimes less serious than felonies; minor criminal acts
nominate	name as a candidate
naturalization	act of becoming a citizen of a country
oath	sacred promise
objections	reasons for being against
obligation	legal or moral duty
original jurisdiction	power to try a case first
originate	begin; start
pardon	order to release a person convicted of a crime
penalty	punishment

personal liberties	individual rights
petition	written statement supported by the signatures of citizens that are either for or against some action taken or about to be taken by our elected officials
plaintiff	person who brings an action at law
pocket veto	President's act of allowing time limit to run out on a bill after Congress has adjourned
polls	voting places
poll tax	voting tax collected to pay cost of holding an election
posterity	those who are born after us
presiding officer	chairman; person who conducts a meeting
primary election	public election held before the general election to nominate candidates within a political party to run in the general election
principal	chief; first
privilege	special right
proceedings	manner of performing duties
prohibit	forbid
proportion	relation; ratio
prosecute	accuse and attempt to prove guilty
purchase	buy
qualification	requirement
quarter	supply room and board for
quorum	number of members that must be present to carry on business
ratify	agree to; adopt; accept
redress	correction
register	place name on list of qualified voters
regulate	control
repeal	cancel; end
reprieve	order to delay or suspend the carrying out of a court sentence
resign	quit, give up a job
restriction	limitation; control
revenue	money received from taxation or any other source
revise	change and improve
secede	withdraw
seizure	arrests or confiscations; taking of one's belongings

session	time spent in meeting
slander	damaging statements made against a person
sole	one, only
standard	definite scale
state of the union message	address made by the President to Congress at the beginning of each session recommending needed laws
subpoena	court order forcing a witness to appear in court
successor	person who follows a preceding office-holder in his office
suffrage	right to vote
supreme	highest
suspend	take away; end
sustain	uphold
taxes	money paid to the government and used for its operation
temporary	not permanent
term	period of time
territory	land region belonging to a government
testify	bear witness
tranquillity	peace
treaty	agreement between nations
unanimous	all; 100 percent
vacancy	a public office not held by anyone
valid	in effect; acceptable
verdict	decision; ruling
veto	refuse to sign, along with act of returning objections
void	expired; no longer existing
warrant	written court order allowing the arrest, search, and seizure of certain persons or certain property
welfare	well-being; good condition
writs of assistance	general search warrants

The Executioner's Song

The following text should be read in the context of topics 17 and 18 of *Modern World 2.* It is taken from Norman Mailer's *The Executioner's Song,* Arrow Books, London 1980, dealing with the life and death of Gary Gilmore, ". . . who, in the summer of 1976, cold-bloodedly gunned down two men . . . For those murders he was sentenced to death, in a country where there hadn't been an execution for a decade. Normally, his sentence would have been almost automatically changed to life imprisonment. But Gary Gilmore insisted that the original sentence be carried out – the ensuing battle and victory made him a media star, turning both his life and his death into a marketable commodity, a grisly media event." (*The Executioner's Song,* blurb)

INTERVIEWER As far as we can tell from your prison record, you've been blocked up almost continuously since you entered reform school, and that was twenty-two years ago. It's as if you never saw any choice but to live out a criminal destiny.

GILMORE Yea, that's kind of a way of putting it. In fact, that's very nicely put.

INTERVIEWER What got you started thinking like a criminal?

GILMORE Probably going to reform school.

INTERVIEWER But you must have done things to get yourself sent there.

GILMORE Yea, I was about fourteen when I went to reform school and, ah, thirteen when I started getting locked up.

INTERVIEWER What had you done to get locked up at thirteen?

GILMORE Well, I started out stealing cars . . . but, ah, I guess my first felonies were probably burglaries, house burglaries. I used to burglarize houses on my paper route.

INTERVIEWER Why? What were you after?

GILMORE Why? Well, I wanted guns, mainly. A lot of people keep guns in their homes and, well . . . that's what I was primarily looking for.

INTERVIEWER How old were you then? Eleven? Twelve? Why did you want guns?

GILMORE Well, see, in Portland, at that time, there was a gang. I don't know if you ever heard of it – probably not. But, man, I figured that, well, I would like to be in the Broadway gang. And I figured the best way to get in was to go down and hang around Broadway and sell 'em guns. I knew they wanted guns. I mean, I – I don't even know if the gang existed . . . it may have been a myth. But I heard about 'em, you know? So I thought, I wanted to be a part of an outfit like that . . . the Broadway boys.

INTERVIEWER But instead you got caught and sent to reform school?

GILMORE Yeah, the MacLaren School for Boys, in Woodburn, Oregon.

INTERVIEWER Was it bad at Woodburn? How did you fit in there?

GILMORE Man, that place made me think that was the only way to live. The guys in there I looked up to, they were tough, they were hipsters – this was the Fifties – and they seemed to run everything there. The staff were local beer-drinking guys that put in their hours, and they didn't care if you did this or did that. They had a few psyche doctors there, too. Psychoanalysis was a big thing then. They would come in and they would show you their ink-blot tests and they would ask you all kinds of questions, mostly related to sex. And look at ya funny and . . . things like that.

INTERVIEWER How did you feel when you were released from Woodburn?

GILMORE I came out looking for trouble. Thought that's what you're supposed to do. I felt slightly superior to everybody else 'cause I'd been in reform school. I had a tough-guy complex, that sort of smart-aleck juvenile-delinquent attitude. *Juvenile delinquent*– remember that phrase? Sure dates me, don't it? Nobody could tell me anything. I had a ducktail haircut, I smoked, drank, shot heroin, smoked weed, took speed, got into fights, chased and caught pretty little broads. The Fifties were a hell of a time to be a juvenile delinquent. I stole and robbed and gambled and went to Fats Domino and Gene Vincent dances at the local halls. . . .

Good stuff, thought Farrell. A good beginning.

Farrell and Schiller agreed that the trick was to get Gary to talk truly about the murders.

GILMORE April got in the truck and, man, she turned the radio on real loud and moved right over beside me and told me she didn't want to go home, and I told her, Well, look, I'll keep you out all night, if you want. So I drove down to the place where I'd bought my truck and I talked to those guys about the financial arrangements. I give 'em my Mustang as the down payment and we drank some booze and just kind of made a loose arrangement about the truck, they were more or less just holding my guns for me, and, uh, I kept one pistol with me, the loaded one, and I signed the papers and took ownership of the truck and left my Mustang there, and then I was driving around with April and we got out into Orem and I pulled around the corner to this service station and it looked fairly deserted. That's what I guess drew my attention to it. I just drove around the corner and parked and told April to stay in the truck. I'd be back in a moment. And I went over to the gas station and told Jensen to give me the money, and he did, and I told him, well, come on in the bathroom and get down on the floor, and it was pretty quick. I didn't let him know it was coming or anything. It was just a 22, so I shot him twice in rapid succession, to make sure that he was not in any pain or that he wasn't left half alive or anything. And, and, I left there and I drove to, uh, I don't know just where that Sinclair station was, but I drove back to the main drag. State Street, I guess it is, and I went into Albertson's and bought some potato chips and different things to take to a movie and half a case of beer and some things that April wanted to eat.

INTERVIEWER Now, one thing. When you stopped at the gas station, did you have any intention of either robbing Jensen or killing him?

GILMORE I had the intention of killing him.

INTERVIEWER When did that concept form in your mind? To kill somebody –

GILMORE I can't say. It had been building all week. That night I knew I had to open a valve and let something out and I didn't know exactly what it would be and I wasn't thinking I'll do this or I'll do that, or that 'll make me feel better. I just knew something

was happening in me and that I'd let some of the steam off and, uh, I guess all this sounds pretty vicious.
INTERVIEWER No. No. Did Jensen say anything to annoy you?
GILMORE No, not at all.
INTERVIEWER What prompted you to leave the truck and go into the office where Jensen was?
GILMORE I don't really know.
INTERVIEWER What do you mean by that?
GILMORE I mean, I don't really know. I said the place looked deserted. It just seemed appropriate.
INTERVIEWER Apparently, killing Jensen didn't do anything to take the pressure off. Why did you go out the next night and kill Bushnell?
GILMORE I don't know, man. I'm impulsive. I don't think.
INTERVIEWER You killed him the same way you'd killed Jensen the night before – ordering him to lie down on the floor, then firing point-blank into his head. Did you think killing Bushnell would give you some kind of relief you didn't get with Jensen?
GILMORE I told you, I wasn't thinking. What I do remember is an absence of thought. Just movements, actions. I shot Bushnell, and then the gun jammed – them fucking Automatics! And I thought, man, this guy's not dead. I wanted to shoot him a second time, because I didn't want him to lie there half dead. I didn't want him in pain. I tried to jack the mechanism and get the gun working again, and shoot him again, but it was jammed, and I had to get my ass out of there. I jacked the gun into shape again but too late to do anything for Mr. Bushnell. I'm afraid he didn't die immediately. When I ordered him to lie down, I wanted it to be quick for him. There was no chance, no choice for him. That sounds cold. But you asked.
INTERVIEWER Was there any difference in the way you approached the two killings?
GILMORE No, not really. You could say it was a little more certain that Mr. Bushnell was going to die.
INTERVIEWER Why?
GILMORE Because it was already a fact that Mr. Jensen had died, and so the next one was more certain.
INTERVIEWER Was the second killing easier than the first?
GILMORE Neither one of 'em were hard or easy.
INTERVIEWER Had you ever had any dealings of any kind with either of those men?
GILMORE No.
INTERVIEWER Well, what led you to the City Center Motel, where Bushnell worked? We're just trying to understand the quality of this rage you speak of. It wasn't a rage that might have been vented in sex?
GILMORE I don't want to mess with questions that pertain to sex. I think they're cheap.
INTERVIEWER But if, on the night you killed Bushnell, you had wound up with a friendly girl who could offer you beer and company and a relaxing time, wouldn't that have helped you feel better?
GILMORE I don't want to answer that question.

INTERVIEWER You seem to find it easier talking about murder than sex.
GILMORE That's your judgment.
INTERVIEWER Why did you kill Jensen and Bushnell?
GILMORE There is so much similarity between Jensen and Bushnell: both mid 20's in age, both family men, both Mormon missionaries. Perhaps the murders of these men were meant to occur.
To answer your question: I killed Jensen and Bushnell because I did not want to kill Nicole. (Gilmore's girl friend who had let him down the week prior to the killings.)

The execution
Ron Stanger's first impression was how many people were in the room. God, the number of spectators. Executions must be a spectator sport. It really hit him even before his first look at Gary, and then he was thankful the hood was not on yet. That was a relief. Gilmore was still a human being, not a hooded, grotesque thing, and Ron realized how he had been preparing himself for the shock of seeing Gary with his face concealed in a black bag. But, no, there was Gary staring at the crowd with an odd humor in his face. Stanger knew what he was thinking. "Anybody who knows somebody is going to get an invite to the turkey shoot."
An official came up to Vern and said Gary wanted to speak to him. Vern walked over into the light that was on Gary, and his nephew looked up at him with those baby-blue eyes of his, and Vern felt he'd like to pull him out of that chair, just pull him out of that chair and make him free again. Vern was feeling a great deal of emotion. He didn't want him in that chair, really.
Gary said, "Look, take this watch. I don't want anybody to have it but Nicole." He had broken it and taped it with the hands set at 7:49. Now, he handed it to Vern. Must have been holding it all this while. Then Gary said, "I want you to promise you'll see to it that Nicole is taken care of." How in the world Gary figured he could take care of her, Vern didn't know, but Gary had to ask somebody. They shook hands and Gary started to squeeze his hand, right there in the chair as if he could crush Vern's knuckles.
Vern went back to his place behind the line and thought of the conversation he'd had weeks before when Gary asked him and Ida to be witnesses, and Vern had said, "I don't want Ida to see it," and Gary said, "but I want *you* there, Vern."
"I don't know whether I can take it or not," Vern had said, "I don't think I can." Gary had said, "Well, I want you there."
"Why? Vern asked. "Why do you want me?"
"Well, Vern," Gary said, "I want to show you. I've already shown you how I live" – he gave his most mocking smile – "and I'd like to show you how I can die." Vern thought all this now must be part of what he had said then because, back behind the line, feeling Gary's hand still on his, Vern wanted to tell him, "That was so good, Gary, what you just did."
Then the Warden said, "Do you have anything you'd like to say?" and Gary looked up at the ceiling and hesitated, then said, "Let's do it." That was it. The most pronounced amount of courage, Vern decided, he'd ever seen, no quaver, no throatiness, right down the line. Gary had looked at Vern as he spoke.
Father Meersman finished giving Gary Gilmore the last rites. As they came forward

with the hood, Gilmore said to him, “Dominus vobiscum.” Father Meersman didn't know how to describe his emotion. Gary couldn't have said anything that brought back more of an automatic response. This was the greeting Father Meersman had given to the people again and again over the ten years and twenty and thirty since he had become a priest. “Dominus vobiscum,” he would say at Mass and the response would come back, „Et cum spiritu tuo.”

So now, when Gilmore said Dominus vobiscum, Father Meersman answered like an altar boy, “Et cum spiritu tuo,” and as the words came out of his mouth, Gary kind of grinned and said, “There'll always be a Meersman.”

Three or four men in red coats came up and put the hood on Gilmore's head. Nothing was said after that.

Absolutely nothing said. They put a waist strap on Gilmore, and a head strap, and Father Meersman began to think of how when they were first strapping him in the chair, Gilmore had wanted water and Father Meersman had given him water for the throat that was too dry. Then he had wanted another drink.

Now, the doctor was beside him, pinning a white circle on Gilmore's black shirt, and the doctor stepped back. Father Meersman traced the big sign of the cross, the last act he had to perform. Then, he, too, stepped over the line, and turned around, and looked back at the hooded figure in the chair.

Gary's body looked calm. Ron could not believe the calm he saw on that man. Gilmore was so strong in his desire to die right, that he didn't clench his fist as the count began.

Vern just heard a great big *WHAM!* When it happened, Gary never raised a finger. Didn't quiver at all. His left hand never moved, and then, after he was shot, his head went forward, but the strap held his head up, and then the right hand slowly rose in the air and slowly went down as if to say. “That did it, gentlemen.” Schiller thought the movement was as delicate as the fingers of a pianist raising his hand before he puts it down on the keys. The blood started to flow throught the black shirt and came out into the white pants and started to drop on the floor between Gary's legs, and the smell of gunpowder was everywhere. Then, the lights went down, and Schiller listened to the blood drip. He was not certain he could hear it drip, but he felt it, and with that blood, the life in Gilmore's body seemed so lift off him like smoke.

Ron closed his eyes and when he opened them again, the blood was a pool in Gary's lap, running to his feet and covering his tennis shoes, those crazy red, white and blue tennis shoes he always wore in Maximum. The shoelaces were now blooded over.

A doctor came along with a stethoscope and shook his head. Gilmore wasn't dead yet.

They waited about twenty seconds. Then the doctor went up again, and Father Meersman came up, and Sam Smith, and the doctor put the stethoscope to Gary's arm once more, turned to Sam, and nodded. Sam Smith unloosened the waist strap, slid Gilmore out from anderneath the head strap, and looked behind the body at the shot pattern where the holes came through.

Stanger was furious. The moment Gilmore was shot, everybody should have been walked out, and not served for a party to all this. Even as Sam was examining the body, Gary fell over into Meersman's hands. The padre had to hold the head while

Sam went fishing all over Gilmore's back to locate the exit wounds. Blood started coming into Meersman's hands, and dripped through his fingers, and Vern began to weep. Then Father Meersman wept. An officer finally came around and said to the people standing behind the line, "Time for you to leave." Schiller walked out saying to himself, "What have we accomplished? There aren't going to be less murders."

Vern, Bob Moody, Ron Stanger, and Larry Schiller got into a car and drove over to the Administration Building. During that minute, they discussed whether or not to issue a press statement ahead of the Warden.

Stanger said, "I think we ought to. What do you say, Larry? Schiller replied, "We have no obligation. The first person who gets there is the first person the press will talk to," and Stanger said, "Let's beat the Warden to the punch."

Vern said, "Can you answer questions about the execution, Larry? I don't want to talk about that."

The press conference was being held on the second floor of the Administration Building in a large conference chamber that looked like a courtroom. It was already as crowded as the Board of Pardons Hearing, same bedlam of media, cameras and crazy white light, people pushing to get in, close to 100 degrees inside. No room to breathe.

When they reached the stage, Schiller said to Vern, "Why don't you talk first?" and Vern sat on a chair to rest his aching leg.

He did not speak long. "It was very upsetting to me," Vern said, "but he got his wish, he did die . . . and he died in dignity. That's all I have to say."

Bob Moody told them: "I think it's a very brutal, cruel kind of a thing, that I would only hope that we could take a good and better look at ourselves, our society and our systems. Thank you."

Assignments

1. Sum up what the text says about Gilmore's youth and the killings. Do you think the KILLINGS had their cause in his experiences as an adolescent?
2. Gilmore says the reason for the murders was that he didn't want to kill his girlfriend Nicole. What does this argument – if it contains the truth – suggest about his psychic state at the time of the murders, and about the structure of his personality?
3. Some of the persons witnessing Gilmore's execution expressed their disagreement with capital punishment. Do you think Gilmore deserved the death penalty?
4. Gilmore's case was marketed by the media and his execution turned into a public spectacle because he was the first murderer to insist on his own execution. What is your opinion of the 'media event'? (press interviews with the killer; large numbers of spectators present at the execution, a press conference afterwards, etc.) What does it tell us about people's interests? What do you think of the role of large sections of the media?

THE NUCLEAR HOLOCAUST

A Forget it, Lad, Forget it!

Young Stan comes around yesterday about tea-time – you know my grandson Stan? He's a Polytechnic student, just turned twenty, as smart as his dad was at the same age. Stan's all out to be a commercial artist and do them big coloured posters for the hoardings. Doesn't answer to 'Stan', though – says it's 'common'; says he's either 'Stanley' or he's nothing.

Stan's got a bagful of big, noble ideas; all schemed out carefully, with what he calls 'captions' attached.

Well, I can't say nothing against big, noble ideas. I was a redhot Labour-man myself for a time, forty years ago now, when the Kayser's war ended and the war-profiteers began treading us ex-heroes into the mud. But that's all over long ago – in fact, Labour's got a damn sight too respectable for my taste! Worse than Tories, most of their leaders is now – especially them that used to be the loudest in rendering 'We'll Keep the Red Flag Flying Still". They're all Churchwardens now, or country gents, if they're not in the House of Lords.

Anyhow, yesterday Stan came around, about a big Ban-the-Bomb march all the way across England to Trafalgar Square. And couldn't I persuade a few of my old comrades to form a special squad with a banner marked 'First World War Veterans Protest Against the Bomb'? He wanted us to head the parade, ribbons, crutches, wheel-chairs and all.

I put my foot down pretty hard. 'No, Mr Stanley,' I said politely, 'I regret as I can't accept your kind invitation.'

'But why?' says he. 'You don't want another war, Grandfather, do you? You don't want mankind to be annihilated? This time it won't be just a few unlucky chaps killed, like Uncle Arthur in the First War, and Dad in the Second . . . It will be all mankind.'

'Listen, young 'un,' I said. 'I don't trust nobody who talks about mankind – not parsons, not politicians, nor anyone else. There ain't no such thing as "mankind", not practically speaking there ain't.'

'Practically speaking, Grandfather,' says young Stan, 'there *is.* Mankind means all the different nations lumped together – us, the Russians, the Americans, the Germans, the French, and all the rest of them. If the bomb goes off, everyone's finished.'

'It's not going off,' I says.

'But it's gone off twice already – at Hiroshima and Nagasaki,' he argues, 'so why not again? The damage will be definitely final when it *does* go off.'

I wouldn't let Stan have the last word. 'In the crazy, oldfashioned war in which I lost my foot,' I said, a bit sternly, 'the Fritzes used poison gas. They thought it would help 'em to break throught at Wipers. But somehow the line held, and soon our factories were churning out the same stinking stuff for us to use on them. All right, and now what about Hitler's war?'

'What about it?' Stan asks.

'Well,' I says, 'everyone in England was issued an expensive mask in a smart-looking case against poison-gas bombs dropped from the air – me, your Dad, your Ma, and yourself as a tiny tot. But how many poison-gas bombs were dropped on London, or on Berlin? Not a damned one! Both sides were scared stiff. Poison gas had got too deadly. No mask in the market could keep the new sorts out. So there's not going to be no atom bombs dropped neither, I tell you, Stanley my lad; not this side of the Hereafter! Everyone's scared stiff again.'

'Then why do both sides manufacture quantities of atom bombs and pile them up?' he asks.

'Search me,' I said, 'unless it's a clever way of keeping up employment by making believe there's a war on. What with bombs and fall-out shelters, and radar equipment, and unsinkable aircraft-carriers, and satellites, and shooting rockets at the moon, and keeping up big armies – takes two thousand quid nowadays to maintain a soldier in the field, I read the other day.

'Your argument has a bad flaw, Grandfather. The Russians don't need to worry about full employment.'

'No,' said I, 'perhaps they don't. But their politicians and commissars have to keep up the notion of a wicked Capitalist plot to wipe out the poor workers. And they have to show that they're well ahead in the Arms Race. Forget it, lad, forget it! Mankind, which is a term used by maiden ladies and bunpunchers, ain't going to be annihilated by no atom bomb. Only fear can keep the peace. The United Nations are a laugh, and you know it. So thank your lucky stars that the Russians have H-bombs and that the Yanks have H-bombs, stacks of 'em, enough to blow your "mankind" up a thousand times over; and that everyone's equally respectful of everyone else, though not on regular visiting terms.'

I stopped, out of breath, and Dodger takes Stan by the hand. 'You know what's right for *you,* lad,' he says. 'So don't listen to your Grand-dad. Don't be talked out of your beliefs! He's one of the Old and Bold, but maybe he's no wiser nor you and I.'

Adapted from: Robert Graves: "Christmas Truce" in *The Shout And Other Stories,* Penguin Books 1978.

B Peter Porter, 1929–

Your Attention Please

The Polar DEW has just warned that
A nuclear rocket strike of
At least one thousand megatons
Has been launched by the enemy
Directly at our major cities.
This announcement will take
Two and a quarter minutes to make,
You therefore have a further
Eight and a quarter minutes
To comply with the shelter
Requirements published in the Civil
Defence Code – section Atomic Attack.

A specially shortened Mass
Will be broadcast at the end
Of this announcement –
Protestant and Jewish services
Will begin simultaneously –
Select your wavelength immediately
According to instructions
In the Defence Code. Do not
Take well-loved pets (including birds)
Into your shelter – they will consume
Fresh air. Leave the old and bed-
ridden, you can do nothing for them.
Remember to press the sealing
Switch when everyone is in
The shelter. Set the radiation
Aerial, turn on the geiger barometer.
Turn off your Television now.
Turn off your radio immediately
The Services end. At the same time
Secure explosion plugs in the ears
Of each member of your family. Take
Down your plasma flasks. Give your children
The pills marked one and two
In the C. D. green container, then put
Them to bed. Do not break
The inside airlock seals until
The radiation All Clear shows
(Watch for the cuckoo in your
perspex panel), or your District
Touring Doctor rings your bell.
If before this, your air becomes
Exhausted or if any of your family
Is critically injured, administer
The capsules marked 'Valley Forge'
(Red pocket in No. 1 Survival Kit)
For painless death. (Catholics
Will have been instructed by their priests
What to do in this eventuality.)
This announcement is ending. Our President
Has already given order for
Massive retaliation – it will be
Decisive. Some of us may die.

Remember, statistically
It is not likely to be you.
All flags are flying fully dressed
On Government buildings – the sun is shining.
Death is the least we have to fear.
We are all in the hands of God,
Whatever happens happens by His Will.
Now go quickly to your shelters.

From: *The Oxford book of war poetry,* ed. by Jon Stallworthy, Book Club Associates, London 1984.

Last Word

By Robert Sheckley

'Sunlight will
once again break through,

HOW IT MIGHT HAPPEN

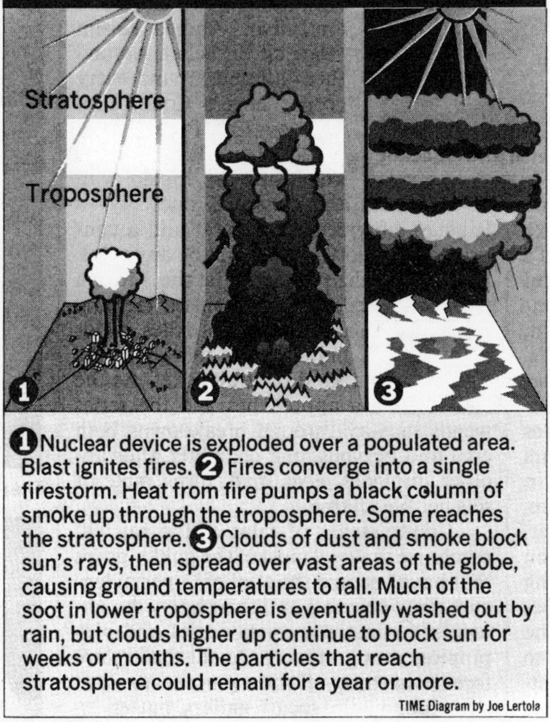

❶ Nuclear device is exploded over a populated area. Blast ignites fires. ❷ Fires converge into a single firestorm. Heat from fire pumps a black column of smoke up through the troposphere. Some reaches the stratosphere. ❸ Clouds of dust and smoke block sun's rays, then spread over vast areas of the globe, causing ground temperatures to fall. Much of the soot in lower troposphere is eventually washed out by rain, but clouds higher up continue to block sun for weeks or months. The particles that reach stratosphere could remain for a year or more.

TIME Diagram by Joe Lertola

Source: *Time,* December 24, 1984.

bringing with
it the deadly variety
of climates,
plants, and animals that
characterized
our unhappy past.'

This is, frankly, an appeal. But I am going to preface it with a little history. Humanity's most crucial day, as we all know, was April 5, 2084, when a multiheaded atomic missile was detected on military radar screens. Its point of launch has never been determined. Its target was the United Nations satellite in orbit above the equator.

The Americans launched their own atomic missiles to destroy it, unfortunately neglecting to tell anyone else what they were doing. The Russians, misinterpreting the American action, launched their own missiles to take out the American missiles. The British followed, then the French, East Germans, Poles, and then everyone else. All claimed to be acting solely in self-defense. They were still arguing about this when the missiles converged above our atmosphere and exploded.

The resulting multimegaton shock wave dissipated harmlessly in space. The expected worldwide fallout of lethal radiation did not take place, and the sheer intensity of the explosion broke down the radiation into gravitons and antigravitons, the ultimate constituents of matter. The gravitons fell harmlessly to Earth, while the antigravitons whirled off into space.

But there was another danger. The estimated 500 megations that exploded in the earth's atmosphere produced a cloud of smoke that covered the earth to a height of some 20 miles and was as impervious to sunshine as are the clouds above Venus. The long nuclear winter had begun.

The earth was plunged into darkness. Temperatures plummeted. Bodies of water smaller than the Caspian Sea froze solid. Blizzards raged over the earth, with death and destruction following in their wake. Snow fell endlessly from the black skies. Without sunshine, plant life was doomed. Without plant life, all animals would die including man himself. Mankind searched desperately for a solution before the dwindling supplies of food and fuel ran out.

It was Luigi Franzetti, an Italian biochemist, who discovered a mutated subspecies of Norway rat capable of sustaining itself indefinitely, without any apparent food source, in subzero conditions. This rat produced a unique enzyme in its liver which, combined with water, yielded a complex protein capable of sustaining life. In its synthetic form, this substance came to be known as Food Type One.

Food Type One now sustains our civilization. Its flavors and textures can be manipulated in the laboratory to suit any taste. Since it has a high content of volatile oil, it can also be used for heating and lighting. In its secondary forms it can be fabricated into durable building materials for houses and vehicles. Waste products from these manufacturing procedures can be reprocessed and extruded into threads of amazing resilience and durability. Fabric woven from this material has a sheen and texture that reminds some of our elder citizens of a luxurious substance once known as silk. Ease of production ensures that food, shelter, and clothing are available to all, thus making possible our present peace-loving civilization.

Our psychohistorians believe they have discovered the probable cause for the savage cruelties of our past. They are convinced that the great variety of foods and climates had a continually unsettling effect upon mankind. This fatal variety, combined with the well-known deleterious effects of daily sunshine, were responsible for the racial, political, and ideational diversity that drove the human race to the wars and violence that plagued it for so many thousands of years.

With the faultless wisdom of hindsight, we now know that the synergy of direct sunlight and other environmental factors – our predecessors' sparing use of food additives, their insistence on wearing clothing of natural fibers, and their fanatical adherence to jogging and aerobic dancing, both of which were once thought to be health-promoting rituals – had a subversive effect on human civilization. Fortunately, we realized in time the value of eschewing natural foods and spending as much time as possible basking in the beneficial radiation of our television screens. As a consequence, we have enjoyed remarkable health as a society, so much so that it is a newsworthy event when anyone succumbs to the uncommon cold before his second century of life. Shielded from the lifesapping energy of our sun, we have managed to enjoy an era of peace and prosperity unprecedented in the history of our planet.

I come now to the purpose of this essay. In recent years our scientists have found that our dense cloud cover is beginning to dissipate. Unless something is done and done soon, we will lose our protective cover. Sunlight will once again break through, bringing with it the deadly variety of climates, plants, and animals that characterized our unhappy past. Mankind will be plunged once again into cutthroat competition, unbridled individualism, and endless war. This is not mere sensationalism! Steps must be taken to preserve our clouds *now,* not later. Otherwise, it will be too late. The clouds may seem eternal, but believe me, they are not.

Therefore when you local Smiling Lady in Black comes to your door and asks you to contribute to the Fund to Protect Our Clouds, give generously, and help support this vital cause. Give all you can, and wear with pride the small black-and-white button that bears the fund's proud motto: KEEP EARTH DARK!

Robert Sheckley is the well-known sciencefiction writer who, until recently, has been living in sunny Costa del Sol, Spain.

From: *Omni,* February 1985

Assignments

1. Outline the different views of Grandfather and Stan about nuclear weapons. (Text A)
2. Whose opinion is shown in the text as being right? Why isn't this surprising?
3. Which view do *you* prefer, and why?

4. Are there any arguments against piling up nuclear bombs and using them as deterrents which are not mentioned in the text?
5. What is Peter Porter's "poem" a satire on?
6. How is the satirical effect achieved?
7. Porter's scenario shows how – as soon as a nuclear war has started – the countries involved can do nothing against the impending holocaust. Is it therefore time for the countries of the West to participate in America's SDI (= Strategic Defense Initiative) program, which intends to establish a shield of laser weapons in space against nuclear missiles?
8. Sum up the contents of text C.
9. Which literary genre does this "history" belong to (besides being a sf story, of course), and why?
10. The story's crucial problem is based on a scientific assumption. Describe it by referring to the *Time* diagram above.